HOLDING HIS HAND

HOPE WHEN LIFE
FEELS HOPELESS

HOLDING
HIS
HAND

JEFF & NANCY COLE

Dedication

Immanuel—how could we not dedicate this book to You!

Thank You for giving us this story to share. Thank You for Your love,
Your guidance, getting us on track, and getting us back on track
when needed. We are so grateful for You!

Contents

CHAPTER 1

Unprepared

NANCY

The alarm dings, and I reach to shut it off. I have been awake for a couple of hours already, planning out what will be an unusual day. I want it to go smoothly, or as smoothly as it can when you have a three-year-old son with autism, a nine-month-old baby, and a husband who's about to have surgery.

I have been over Keith's tonsillectomy preoperative and post-op instructions several times, and I remind myself this is a simple outpatient procedure. The pain meds are ready, and the freezer is stocked with ice cream to soothe his sore throat.

Our caregiver's light is shining into the hallway from under her door—Diane will be ready if the kids wake up early.

Our son, Billy, is on the autism spectrum and has many challenges. Every sound, activity, and change in routine—even settling down and sleeping—is difficult. I hadn't realized how much more difficult life is for him until Riley was born. Riley is a typical baby, and things seem to come effortlessly for her.

That being said, managing the two of them can be pretty tricky, especially in public places. When Billy gets overwhelmed, which can happen quickly, he goes into fight-or-flight mode. Some days, even a ten-minute trip to the grocery store is too much, and once he's in overload, there is no quick recovery. I've had to abandon far too many full shopping carts to get us out of the store as quickly as possible.

After nine months of being a single parent most of the time—given Keith's work schedule—I felt the strain of trying to do too much by myself. A month ago, we hired Diane as live-in help with Billy, and she has lessened my pressure. I even grocery shop by myself now.

After checking on the kids one more time, Keith and I slip out the front door of our home.

It's still dark as we pull into a parking spot near the entrance to the outpatient surgery center.

After the paperwork and pre-op procedures are done, they wheel my husband down the hall and around the corner. The surgery can soon be checked off the to-do list.

The sun is just coming up as I walk out of the hospital. I hope to make it home before the kids wake up. Since they are now both sleeping through the night, my mornings with them are a favorite time. And since the hospital will notify me when Keith's out of surgery, why not spend the morning with the kids?

I tiptoe into the still-silent house and start the coffee, hoping to grab a quick cup before the daily routine begins. As I sit at the kitchen table sipping my coffee, my shoulders relax, and I take in the tranquil view of the nature preserve outside our large windows. We hope to relocate soon for Keith's new job—with fewer hours, less traveling, and more family time. While I'm grateful for that, I'll sure miss the family of raccoons that visits us nightly.

My husband's current job requires not only domestic travel but international travel over 40 percent of the time. With Billy's autism and a new baby in the house, we have set out to find Keith a job that doesn't require travel—and he's already had one interview, in the San Francisco area. We're both from California and look forward to returning to our home state.

In the meantime, Diane helps me manage Billy's care and the needs of sweet baby Riley along with taking care of the household tasks and chores. Checking this surgery off the list means we can move forward with our plans. The surgery will relieve my husband's sleep apnea and snoring. Once he recovers, he can fly to California for his final interview. The future is looking good.

The sound of Billy at the baby gate stirs me from my coffee daydream. Soon Riley joins us, and we start our morning routine of dressing and breakfast. I do a quick workout on the treadmill while watching a *Barney* episode (not my choice) followed by a quick shower. I want to be ready by midmorning in case the surgery is quicker than anticipated. I wash the dishes and then settle onto the couch to read books with Billy and Riley while waiting for the call to let me know my husband is in recovery and will soon be ready to come home.

The phone ringing interrupts our fourth time reading *Blue Hat, Green Hat*. A calm operating-room nurse tells me there were complications during the surgery and my husband has lost a lot of blood. My heart pounds hard as I walk toward the kitchen. I must have misheard her.

"He's okay though, right?" I barely give her time to answer before asking again, "He is going to be okay, isn't he?"

"He is still in surgery, but he is stable," she replies robotically.

I have a difficult time trying to sort out what I'm being told and *not* being told. Her refusal to offer details indicates that things are terribly wrong. I was only waiting on the call to pick him up, not to hear about complications.

The nurse asks if I would like to speak with the surgeon.

"Yes!" I stop pacing and lean against the back of the couch to brace myself.

"There have been some complications." The doctor repeats what the nurse had just said. "And your husband has lost a lot of blood. Do you have someone who can drive you to the hospital?"

I know then the situation is bad.

He tells me they have moved him from the outpatient center to the hospital's main operating room. I hang up, grab my purse, and slip into my shoes. Diane appears at the top of the stairs just in time for me to tell her I need to go.

During the drive, I replay the phone conversation over and over while dialing my mom's number. She answers after only half a ring.

I can barely speak, and I say just two words in a shaky voice, "Mom, pray."

"What's wrong?"

I realize I don't even know. "I just know the surgery did not go well."

"I will be praying nonstop. Let me know as soon as you know something," Mom says.

I don't ever really pray myself, but my mom does, and knowing she's praying comforts me.

Halfway to the hospital, I call my friend Tiffini, my friend Beth, and my sister Juli, and ask them to meet me at the hospital.

As I pull into the parking lot, I can barely think. I don't know where to go. I remember the doctor telling me they'd moved him from the outpatient surgical center to the main hospital. I walk through the front doors, barely able to see through my tears. Just nine months ago, my husband and I walked through these doors when I was in labor with Riley. Now I am wandering through the same lobby without any clarity on my husband's condition or direction about where to go. I scan the front desk for help, but no one is there. It is lunchtime, and the volunteer staff is probably on break.

In a panic, I grab the arm of a man walking with his wife to leave the hospital. My voice quivers as I say through my tears, "My husband is here. They brought him here, but I don't know where to go."

They turn around and usher me down the hallway. They ask someone for assistance, and within a few minutes, I am being led through a waiting room into a smaller waiting room.

A huge wave of panic crashes over me as the hospital chaplain joins me to wait. My mind races. I have been in waiting rooms several times while waiting for a relative or good friend to come out of surgery, but I have never been shown to a little room, and never has a chaplain joined me.

While I wait for an update from the surgeon, my sister and friends walk in. I'm relieved to see them but can only stare at the floor and concentrate on breathing.

When the surgeon finally comes in, he sits in the chair next to me. I lean forward and wring my hands, praying he will tell me Keith is okay.

He does not.

CHAPTER 2

Dazed

JEFF

At 5:30 a.m. I try to slip out of bed without waking Charmaine. She was up several times during the night to feed our two-month-old, Jessica, and I want her to sleep as long as possible. When I step from the shower, I hear Jessica crying and see Charmaine pushing off the covers to go take care of her.

I dress quickly, and as I adjust my tie, I think about everything I need to do before Colin's fourth birthday party on Saturday. It's already Tuesday—where does the time go? Charmaine has ordered the cake, and I plan to clean the pool after work today and mow the lawn tomorrow so everything will be ready for our son's party. Charmaine will surely have another list of errands for me when I come home for lunch.

Charmaine loves birthdays, holidays, and really any reason to have family and friends over. She enjoys all the planning and preparation, and she is especially excited for Colin's birthday party this year because he is excited. We've invited friends from his day care, the first time the party guests will be more than just family. Lynn, the day care owner, whom we consider a close friend, will also be at the party. She plans to retire soon and close the day care. Colin will miss her and his friends, but Charmaine has decided to stay home full time with Colin and Jessica.

Before leaving for work, I peek into the room where Charmaine is feeding Jessica. Jessica's eyes are closed, so I lean down and give Charmaine a kiss, then whisper, "I love you. I'll see you at lunch."

After grabbing a coffee from Starbucks, I listen to my favorite radio sports show during my ten-minute drive to work. As I'm always the first to arrive, I open the office, turn off the alarm, turn on the phones, and get the coffee going. Then I settle myself behind my desk and print out the sales reports from the previous day to review. I want to be ready with the numbers before my brother calls. We've been in business together—medical sales—for nineteen years, so we have the routine down.

I'm surprised by how fast the morning flies by, and before I know it, it's already 11:30. I head to the parking lot and consider stopping for takeout in case Charmaine has been too busy with the kids and house to make lunch. But I don't want to show up with food if she has something ready, so I drive straight home.

After I unlock the door, I try to push it open, but the chain lock catches. Through the small crack I see Colin walking toward me still in his pajamas. Panic rises in my chest. There are two things I can count on: Charmaine always unlatching the chain on the door and Colin always being dressed before coming downstairs in the morning.

I race back out to the driveway and grab the garage remote from the car. I wait a couple of painful seconds before the door rises enough for me to duck under the opening. When I enter the house, Colin meets me in the hall.

"Mommy is asleep and won't wake up. But don't worry, Dad! I got crackers and a juice box."

I take the stairs two at a time and run to the main bedroom. She isn't there. I walk down the short hall to Jessica's room and see Charmaine lying on the floor. Her arms are stretched out to her sides. Jessica is asleep in her crib.

I fall on my knees and place my hand on Charmaine's chest. She isn't breathing. I shake her arm. "Charmaine, Charmaine!" I tilt her head back and breathe into her mouth. I feel a rush of air come out, and for a second, I think it's her breath. I do several compressions before running to the bedroom to call 911.

"Nine-one-one. What's your emergency?"

"My wife isn't breathing. I need help."

"Sir, what's your address? Are you with your wife right now?"

"No, there is no phone in there. Please, I really need help. She isn't breathing. Please hurry."

"They are on their way. I can stay with you on the phone."

"I can't. I need to do more CPR. Please hurry!"

I dash back to Charmaine and continue CPR. After a few compressions, I run downstairs to unlock the front door, then sprint back up to Charmaine and do more CPR.

I can't believe this is happening. When I left this morning, she was fine.

Even though it's not working, I continue CPR until I feel a hand on my shoulder and hear a paramedic's voice behind me say, "We've got this."

I call my mom from the phone in the main bedroom.

"Mom, come over right away."

"What's wrong? What's going on?"

"You need to get over here right now."

I hang up and run downstairs to find Colin. He's sitting on the couch and looks so small in his Spider-Man pajamas. I sit next to him, put my arm around him, and turn on the TV. We watch *Dragon Tales* with the volume so low I can barely hear it. I replay the morning in my head. *She was fine, wasn't she? She seemed fine when I said goodbye. Did she fall? She didn't look like she fell. Jessica is in her crib. It looks like she just lay down.*

My thoughts are interrupted by a police officer entering the room. "May I speak to you in the other room?"

When I join her in the dining room, she says, "I just have a few questions. Was your wife ill?"

"No, she was fine. She didn't mention not feeling well."

"What time did you leave this morning?"

"Around six."

"Did you speak with your wife at all during the morning?"

8

"No, I always come home at lunch. I don't usually call her. She knew I was coming home . . . I guess I should have called her."

"You were just doing what you normally do." Her eyes look sympathetic. "It's okay."

It doesn't feel okay.

As the officer finishes off her questions, my parents arrive. The officer steps outside to talk to them.

I turn to another officer and ask her if she can please get my daughter from her crib. She brings Jessica to me, and I hold her a few minutes before giving her to my mom. Then I return to sit with Colin and continue staring at the TV while my mom changes Jessica, then feeds her. I want to be there in case Colin asks me any questions. I also want to keep an eye on him, so he will not go upstairs while they are working on Charmaine. I can hear my dad on the phone. He is probably talking to my brother.

Another police officer comes in to talk with me. We go into the hallway, where he asks the same questions about the morning. I also see an officer in our backyard talking with the gardener.

When that officer comes back in, I overhear him tell his colleague, "He didn't hear or see anything except for a little boy sitting at the table eating."

A few minutes later, another officer walks into the house and asks to speak with me. I answer the same questions again. Then I see several officers talking together while looking at their notebooks.

I look up to see a paramedic coming down the stairs, talking with one of the police officers.

"No trauma," he reports.

Then the paramedic motions to me, and I follow him into the dining room.

"I'm really sorry," he says. "We did everything we could."

CHAPTER 3

Unsatisfactory Explanation

NANCY

"Your husband has a bleeding disorder," the surgeon says softly, "and I need to ask you some questions. We have a team working to stop the bleeding."

As my mind races, he asks me questions that I assume, if I can answer, will help save Keith. The surgeon questions about his health history—which we had been over together by phone two days before the surgery. He asks what he had to eat or drink prior to surgery. When he again mentions a blood-clotting disorder, I cut him off midsentence.

"What about the blood-clotting test they ran this morning? Did it come back normal?" When he doesn't answer, I ask, "Did they not wait for the results before starting the surgery?"

Rather than answer my question, he mumbles, "These things happen," then returns to the operating room to check on him.

I sit and wait for the door to open again, hoping someone else will enter with an update I can understand. Dread settles in my chest, and I'm not sure what I should be doing. I look around the room at my sweet friends gathered here to help. Clearly none of us knows what to say or do. The door could open at any minute, and I'll possibly be given the worst news any wife could ever receive.

My chest feels tight as I turn to the chaplain. "Can we pray?"

My friends look at me, and I know my request seems foreign. I'm not a religious person. I grew up with religion, but it left me feeling very empty and disappointed. In fact, I haven't thought about God at all in the last several years. I go to church on major holidays out of childhood obligation, but that's about it. Does God really even hear prayers? I'm not sure, but right now praying seems like the only thing to do.

The chaplain reaches out, so we all hold hands. As he prays, I don't even listen to the words. I'm just happy to have some of the silence filled by something other than worry. I don't expect much.

But as he prays, something happens. I experience a sensation of deep peace. It is an amazing feeling.

The day continues to be a whirlwind of multiple doctors and surgeons giving us updates. None of them give hope. The most optimistic word I hear is "stable," but it is always followed by "for the moment." My husband is still in trouble.

As the hours tick by, it becomes difficult to keep track of all the doctors. The cycle of people in and out includes four surgeons (three of whom had been called in to assist), the radiologist, and a handful of other specialists. After making brief eye contact, I often look down at the shoes of the person speaking. In my exhaustion, it's easier to keep track of people by their shoes. *Cowboy boots again* or *black loafers*. There is a discussion about the possibility of moving my husband to another hospital with specialized equipment that could better determine the source of the bleeding. That idea is ruled out, however, when his medical team decides he would not survive the trip.

Not knowing how many days I'll be at the hospital, I call my mom—who lives in San Diego—to come help with the kids. She'll arrive tomorrow. Between her and Diane, the kids will be well cared for.

Keith, I'm not so sure of.

At times, after what feels like days—but had only been hours—of sitting and anticipating, the door between the operating room and the small waiting room swings open. I glance up for an update, only to see the surprised look of a nurse who mutters, "I'm sorry, I didn't know anyone was in here." The small waiting room connects to the larger waiting room and is apparently used as a shortcut to give updates to the families in the larger room.

That is where I should be—in the big waiting room. The waiting room where you are not given devastating news.

Still overwhelmed, I again ask the chaplain, "Can we pray?" I am not asking because I believe God will answer my prayers. I don't know much about God. I believe in Him, but since childhood I had learned to view God as more of a ruler or judge. I don't believe He cares about me personally. I only ask to pray because it breaks the silence in the room.

Each time we hold hands and pray, I don't really hear the words, but I do feel peace. These prayers begin to change my mind about God. It's a sense of peace I have never felt in my life. I know it's not coming from my effort. I know it's something much greater than me. And I know it happens each time the chaplain prays. I have a deep sense of knowing I will be okay. I still have no idea whether Keith will live or not, but the peace is not dependent upon the outcome of the surgery. It is simply . . . peace. A peace I have not known before.

In the early evening hours, we are given good news. My husband is out of surgery and stable enough to be moved to ICU. I finally take more than a shallow breath, and we gather our things.

Once we are upstairs in the ICU waiting room, a nurse tells us I'll be able to see him soon. I am so grateful for my friends, who have spent the entire afternoon with me in such an intense situation. Finally, we are able to talk about the day. I am no longer holding my breath while waiting for bad news.

"We should get you something to eat," Tiffini says.

"Nancy, have you had anything to eat today?" Juli asks.

"I can run down to the cafeteria," Beth adds.

As we're discussing food, the same ICU nurse appears. "Nancy, we need to take your husband back to the OR stat. We'd like you to come and see him before we move him. Please come now."

With panic in every part of my body and mind, I follow her through the double doors. When I turn left toward his room, I can see through the glass wall to the team working on him. They are holding pressure on his throat. As I enter the room and walk toward him, I say his name. He shoots up and looks at me through wild eyes. The team lowers him back down and wheels him past me to the elevator and back to the operating room.

These few seconds with him are like a cruel joke. After waiting all day and finally feeling some relief, we must head back to the small room.

Minutes later, the elevator doors open, and all four of us troop silently into the elevator. My mind races as we return to the same small waiting area, and all I can think about is my children, who might lose their daddy.

I try not to panic as I settle back into a chair. Once again, the chaplain prays for the surgeons and for Keith, and we wait. Discussions of dinner are on hold. We are all just trying our best to believe they will save him. The prayers help bring some peace and calm again.

Finally, the surgeon wearing cowboy boots appears in the doorway and tells us Keith is in recovery. They will let us know when he is ready to be moved to ICU. When we do return upstairs to the ICU an hour later, I feel tremendous relief, even though I'm told he suffered a stroke during the surgery. I have no idea what this will mean for our future, but I'm simply grateful he is alive.

CHAPTER 4

In Shock

JEFF

I hear my dad in the kitchen saying over and over again, "No, no, no, it just isn't right."

I have so many questions for the paramedic, but all I manage to stammer out is a vague "W-what happened?"

He gently explains that they don't know, but an autopsy will provide the answers. As he speaks, the reality that Charmaine is actually gone hits home.

Although a part of me expects this news, another part of me was holding on to the hope that they would bring her back. I thank the paramedic, and he puts his arm around me, and we hug.

"It will be okay," I say, even though I cannot imagine *how.*

An officer taps me on the shoulder. "Can I call anyone for you?"

"Please call our church. Charmaine sings in the worship band, so the pastors know her."

Within an hour, a pastor and a few of Charmaine's friends walk into the house.

Soon my home fills up. My brother and my sister-in-law arrive too. The only people I don't see are Charmaine's parents. I have left several messages, but they are still not here.

When the coroner arrives, I take Colin to the backyard, and we sit on the brick wall. I want to be sure he does not see them taking Charmaine from the house. I'm not sure *I* can handle seeing it, so

I know its best if he is sheltered. He is quiet, waiting for me to say something. How do you tell a four-year-old little boy his mommy has died?

As I open my mouth to speak, the words just come. "Colin, Mommy wasn't feeling good. She went to be with Jesus in heaven." I feel peace at this explanation, but also like the words did not come from me.

He gazes up at me, and after a long pause he asks, "When is she coming back?"

"She is staying there, buddy. She'll be in heaven with Jesus always."

"Like Grandpa's dog Sunset?"

I smile. "Yes, just like Sunset."

We sit there until I see the coroner leave with Charmaine. Through the open front door, I can see a group of neighbors gathered on the sidewalk in front of the house.

Colin and I wander back into the house and join everyone in the living room. Jessica is taking a nap upstairs. Food has somehow appeared on the table, and someone makes me a plate and sets it in front of me. I watch people come and go from the living room to the kitchen and back again. Although I appreciate everyone being here, I also just want everyone to go.

I look up to see Charmaine's parents walk through the front door. My mom takes them into the living room, while I take Colin to another room to protect him from hearing the news again. She tells them what happened, and Charmaine's mom lets out a loud, gut-wrenching cry. She is inconsolable. It is hard to hear her in such pain and not know what to do, given my own numbness with crushing pain waiting to rise up just below the surface.

By early evening, I ask everyone to leave. I know they are worried about us, and I appreciate it, but I really need to be alone with my kids.

I start our evening routine. After I give Jessica a bath and bottle, I put her in her crib for the night.

Things with Colin are not quite as easy. He cries when I cannot find his dinosaur pajamas, and then he starts calling for Mommy. I promise him I will find the pajamas, and I do find them at the bottom of the laundry basket. I'm pretty sure laundry was on Charmaine's list for the day.

We settle into bed for some stories.

"I want Mommy to read it—she does the voices."

"I will do the voices tonight."

"But I like the way Mommy reads it."

"I do too, Colin. I do too."

Finally, after reading four books, I ask Colin if he would like to sleep in bed with me. He picks up his stuffed panda and follows me into my bedroom, where I tuck him in.

After Jessica and Colin are both asleep, I walk around the house. I look at the family pictures hanging on the wall. Most are of Colin, me, and Charmaine. Because Jessica is only two months old, there is only one of us with her, on the day she was born. I realize we will not have any other photos of our family all intact.

As I lie in bed, staring up at the ceiling, I replay the day in my head over and over. How did this happen? She was fine last night. She was fine when I left this morning. What happened? She was my person. The person I planned life with. The person I was supposed to be with. She was so happy. She had the family she had always wanted. She had the house she wanted. She's supposed to be here, and she isn't. I move over to her side of the bed and breathe into her pillow. I can smell her shampoo.

Four days ago, we celebrated her thirty-sixth birthday, and we joked about how old we were getting. We talked about how fast time went by and that we couldn't believe Colin was going to be four.

It seemed we had everything except the white picket fence around the yard. I was pretty sure that one day soon we would have that too.

I remember our Mother's Day celebration just a couple weeks ago. The day had been extra special since Charmaine was now a mother of two.

I finally doze off, but then I wake up reaching for her. She isn't there, and again I replay the day in my head. Should I have known? She had seemed more tired since Jessica was born. But having two kids would do that, wouldn't it?

A few minutes after I settle my mind and sleep a little, I can hear Jessica crying. It's 12:45 a.m. I make a bottle and settle into the rocking chair with her. After I change her and rock her a little more, I crawl back in bed with Colin to try to sleep. It is almost impossible to calm down and sleep, but I manage to drift off.

Finally, morning comes, and I hear Jessica crying in her crib. I make a bottle and sit down in the rocking chair to feed her. I had already planned to take the morning off so Charmaine and I could take Jessica to her two-month checkup. After I finish feeding her, I shower and get dressed so I can take her to the pediatrician. I quickly get Colin fed and dressed. He will be going to day care since his usual schedule is still three days a week.

When we pull in to the driveway, he sees his friends playing. He says, "Bye, Dad" as he runs for the backyard.

I'm glad he will be doing something normal today. It does my heart good to see him smile.

Jessica's checkup goes well until I mention to her doctor that her mom died yesterday. I can tell he doesn't know what to say. Neither do I. We just look at each other for a few seconds before talking about Jessica's formula and discussing that it may be the reason Jessica is waking up so much at night. He suggests we switch to a soy-based formula.

On the way home, I swing by the store to pick some up. Standing in the baby aisle, I look at all the moms pushing their shopping carts while looking at toys, bibs, and pacifiers.

Charmaine would have loved doing this with Jessica.

CHAPTER 5

Unexpected Mystery

NANCY

The machines beep, monitoring my husband's heart rate, his medicines, his breathing—although there is a tube down his throat doing that for him. I sit by his bed and notice how still he is. I've never seen him this still. I can hear the sound of his breathing; however, I know it's the tube down his throat and the machine it's connected to that's doing the breathing. He is so still.

I glance at the clock. Almost 9:00 p.m. I look out the window, and although it's dark, the parking lot is brightly lit. I should go home, but I can't make myself leave.

It's been three days since we came in for a simple procedure. Three days of the same thing, the same news. If he survives a week, he will likely live. If the brain swelling continues to decrease, he will likely live. At this point, that's all I want. I cannot think beyond that.

I try to make sense of it all. I replay conversations and try to understand what's happening. I think back to a conversation with a nurse the morning after his surgery.

I arrived at about 6:00 a.m. after trying to sleep for a few hours. Shortly after seven, my friends Beth and Tiffini arrived and handed me a mocha from a local coffee shop.

When the daytime nurses settled in for their shifts, one pulled me into an empty ICU room.

She scanned the rest of the ICU, then her eyes rested on me. "Nancy," she whispered just loud enough for me to hear. "Your husband's surgeon has been placed on administrative leave, and you need to find a new ear, nose, and throat specialist."

What? "I don't understand. Did something happen with my husband's surgery?"

She glanced furtively to the left and right. "I can't explain everything, but I'm keeping a photocopy of Keith's records for you."

I twisted my hands together. She seemed to be sending me a subtle message, but I wasn't picking it up. "Who will be briefing me on my husband's recovery now? What happens next?"

This felt bizarre and like one more string of bad news.

She handed me a list of possible doctors, which I handed to Beth when I rejoined her and Tiffini. Beth and I made calls to see who had immediate availability. After hours of calls, we did not find a single doctor who would take my husband as a patient. Discouragement and helplessness weighed heavily on my shoulders. *I just wanted to help my husband, and now we don't even have a doctor.*

I cannot believe that just a few days ago, we were enjoying Easter Sunday with the kids. We had been to church, since it was Easter, and afterward had taken a whole roll of pictures of the four of us together and of Billy and Riley with their Easter baskets. Riley loved her Easter basket and stuffed bunny.

Being an optimist and not knowing anything about strokes and recovery, I suggest to Beth that we should have the roll of film developed and frame some pictures. When my husband wakes up, I want him to see pictures of his family. We head off to the store to drop off the film and pick up another mocha.

Since Keith may be disoriented when he awakes, I later place the framed photos next to his bed, hoping they'll comfort him.

Although my husband is not able to see the pictures now, they become a conversation starter with the nurses. They are kind, and I hear over and over again, "What a beautiful family" and "Your children are precious."

Yes, they are, and they want their daddy.

My mom and Diane have been looking after the kids day and night. Since Diane moved into our guest room when we hired her a month ago, my mom sleeps in the main bedroom with Riley, and I sleep on the living room couch so I can slip in and out of the house without waking anyone. I typically leave early—by six—and arrive home around midnight. Although I lie there, I don't sleep well. I toss and turn before getting up to shower and head back to the hospital.

I miss the kids terribly, and I determine to try to come home in the afternoons to spend time with them.

Three days pass while waiting for Keith's brain swelling to decrease, and I still can't find an ENT to take over his care—I've tried about thirty doctors, and although they don't say it, they're all concerned about becoming a party in a lawsuit. The hospital doctor fills in, but nothing changes. The only hope I'm given is that if the swelling goes down and he survives the first week, that's a good sign.

I don't know who to trust or what's really going on. I'm certainly not being told the truth about the surgeon, so what else aren't they telling me?

On day four of this routine, I greet my in-laws in the waiting room, then stride into my husband's room. I spot an envelope with my name on it propped against the nurses' whiteboard. I open it and find a note with a business card stapled to the corner. The note reads: *This person has information for you, if you would like to contact him.*

The business card is for an attorney. I look out through the glass wall to see if anyone is watching me, but the nurses at the desk are busy with their paperwork. I shove the note and envelope into my purse.

This note confirms that something strange is going on.

The only doctors I've spoken with are staff ones, and they provide little info, though the nurses are kind and provide me with Keith's vitals. No one mentions our situation. They repeatedly run blood-clotting tests, and I wonder if they are simply trying to corroborate the surgeon's story. Would they go as far as to give Keith something that would cause him to have a clotting problem?

And why did they put the surgeon on administrative leave?

Later that day, as I pace during a shift change, the waiting room phone rings. My father-in-law answers, then turns to me and says, "It's for you."

I'm surprised since the phones inside the waiting room receive calls only from inside the hospital, but I take the receiver and say hello.

"You need to get the best medical malpractice attorney you can find," a male voice says.

That's not what I was expecting to hear. I turn my back on those in the room. "Who is this?"

"I can't tell you that," the mystery man says, "but you need an attorney. It's all in the records."

I'm shocked but try to get more information. "Is there someone you can recommend?"

"No, I can't recommend anyone, but you need one, and as fast as you can."

"Thank you." I hang up and don't say a word to anyone. This all feels like some sinister movie plot. I return to my husband's ICU room, and everything seems like business as usual in the ICU. But nothing seems usual in my heart or mind.

On Saturday, five days since my husband's surgery, friends arrive in town. Beth and Tiffini were kind enough to phone some friends and relatives, and they have come to support us. It's wonderful to see everyone, but overwhelming at the same time.

We do have some amazing friends. Beth and Tiffini keep me caffeinated every day with my favorite café mocha—but with half the chocolate; otherwise, it is too sweet and will leave me feeling weird. I'm always trying to strike the balance between being awake and alert but not jittery and jumpy.

Not a day goes by that these two women are not there for me. Will and Mike, two of our friends from grad school, take our cars to get oil changes. Some friends grab groceries for my kids, and some bring me meals at the hospital.

The overwhelming support convinces me to confide in someone about the mysterious phone call and business card that was left for me. I pull Will and his wife, Anne, aside one day and explain everything.

"What do you think it means?" I ask. "Should I get an attorney?"

Will encourages me to at least speak to one. I'm still not clear how to go about this, so we begin with the note and business card left in my husband's room. Will schedules an appointment for the next day.

CHAPTER 6

Worried Optimist

NANCY

We pull into the parking lot of the attorney's small office. I tear apart a tissue in my hands. I hate leaving the hospital, but I'll do whatever I must to protect my family. If the surgeon did commit malpractice, I'll need help. So far all we know from Will's phone call is that someone involved in the surgery had sent the surgical report and medical records to this personal injury attorney, Mr. Jones.

We sit across from Mr. Jones's desk while he shares what he knows from the records—records provided by the nurse . . . records I haven't seen. I know I need to be there to hear what actually happened, as opposed to what I was told about the surgery. But I also feel a strong urge to run before I throw up.

As I listen, I feel numb. The lawyer has done some digging and found out that the surgeon has a history of mistakes. Mistakes just like the mistakes he made with my husband. In fact, one woman who had received the same surgery as Keith's from the same surgeon was released from the hospital and died at home.

This is bad. Very bad.

Mr. Jones breaks into my thoughts. "Nancy, do you have any questions?"

"I'm sorry, what?"

I try to focus, and my mind is racing with many questions, but I don't know where to start. I cannot think straight. My biggest question is, *Will my husband live?* Since no one can answer that question, none of the others matter as much.

Will leans forward as the attorney reads the report. My husband had a severed carotid artery, and the surgeon tried to cauterize it himself before calling for help. In fact, according to the report, in trying to find and correct the source of the bleeding, he cauterized several arteries.

How did a simple procedure go so wrong? I just want to return to the hospital, to Keith.

I listen as Mr. Jones reads about operating-room nurses finally leaving to get help. I hear about the anesthesiologist saving Keith's life by replacing his total blood volume two and a half times.

As we leave the attorney's office, I'm anxious and shaky. I have nothing to say. I cannot believe this happened. We climb into Will's SUV to head back to the hospital.

Will glances at me. "What happened to your face?"

I reach up and touch my cheek. During the meeting, I had managed to dig my fingernails into my face hard enough to leave marks. It must have hurt, but I didn't feel any pain.

When we arrive back at the hospital, I sit by my husband's bed. Tears fall down my cheeks and onto my T-shirt and lap. I am so numb. I cannot even begin to imagine how this was allowed to happen. We'd simply selected a doctor from our insurance list. How could he have been on the list? If he keeps making mistakes, how is he allowed to continue to do surgeries? Why didn't someone, anyone, who knew this was a strong possibility stop him?

A few days later, Beth and I meet with another medical malpractice attorney and share our story of the surgery.

He glances at his law assistant. "Don't we have other cases against him?"

I look down at the floor and take some deep breaths.

The whole thing feels so overwhelming that I'm almost relieved when we're told that even if I file a lawsuit, it will take a substantial amount of time before anything happens. I don't have it in me to deal with this now anyway. I have enough on my plate as it is.

We return to the hospital, where we are given more bad news. My husband has a high fever caused by an infection. They start him on antibiotics and continue to monitor his temperature. I'm thankful at least that we now have a new doctor. The ICU nurse had made phone calls on our behalf and found an ENT willing to take Keith as a patient.

I doze in the recliner the nurses have provided. Although I try to sleep, I jump at every little sound or movement from outside the room and at the sound of my husband's monitors. At 11:00 p.m., I finally head for home.

I walk into the ICU in the morning and am given more news—both good and bad. The good news is my husband's swelling has gone down and they plan to remove his breathing tube first thing tomorrow morning. I am so excited! When he wakes up, he will be able to speak! I have been so worried about him waking up and not knowing where he is or what happened, and him possibly not having the ability to ask. I'll be able to talk with him, and that comforts me.

But the bad news is that his infection has not improved, and they are bringing in an infectious disease specialist. The good news and bad news almost cancel each other out, and I remind myself that I am an optimistic person. But deep in my heart, I worry about the infection—a hospital-acquired infection—which can be fatal.

CHAPTER 7

Life Goes On

JEFF

The next day after I pick Colin up from day care and as I take Jessica out of her car seat, the phone rings. I wrangle Colin into the house and football-hold Jessica while picking up the phone. It's my mom. She's wondering if I would like to have a family birthday party for Colin at my brother's house. I'd canceled the other party, and I know that for Colin's sake, this is the best plan.

If only Charmaine could be there too.

I carry Jessica to the living room, where Colin is playing with his Hot Wheels. "Colin, we're going to have your birthday party in a couple of days."

"Yay!" Colin raises his hands in the air. "Will I get presents? Will Mom be there?"

"Remember, buddy, Mom's in heaven now. She can't come from heaven. But Grandma and Papa and lots of others will be there."

"Okay." He picks up two cars and smashes them together.

Saturday morning, I try to be excited and upbeat for Colin. On more than one occasion, I zone out, looking out the window, and then pull myself back to reality. Just a few days ago, I was discussing this party with Charmaine. If she were alive, I'd be setting up chairs in the backyard, blowing up the balloons, and tying up the streamers. Now she isn't here to enjoy the thing she loved most—being with family and celebrating.

I hear my name being called, so I snap back to reality again. I go through the motions of eating some cake, thanking everyone, and then heading for home.

That night, Colin sleeps with me again. We both sleep better together. Jessica also sleeps better with her new formula.

On Sunday, I pack the kids up and head to church. We've been going to this church for four years, and it feels safe and right to be there. We sit in the same seats as always. After giving Colin some toys to keep him occupied and feeding Jessica a bottle, I glance over to the worship band. The gap where Charmaine usually stands seems so large. She will miss singing with them.

But then . . . no. She won't. She's with God now—the One she was always singing to. Now she can sing directly to Him. She isn't missing anything, but I am missing her.

At the end of the service, the praise band walks over to us and asks if they can pray. I nod as my eyes well up with tears.

When we return home, I go through the motions of the tasks that must be accomplished, same as any other day. Laundry. Feed and bathe the kids. Play catch with Colin. Every time I wander into the kitchen or our main bedroom, I expect to see Charmaine. I have to remind myself again and again that she isn't here. It's funny that the house seems both full and empty. Full because of the noise Jessica and Colin make, but empty, very empty, without Charmaine.

On Monday morning, I take Charmaine's parents to pick out a casket and a burial plot with me. By late afternoon, I am standing in our closet trying to pick out an outfit and shoes for her. I see the dress she wore for my birthday—it's my favorite. There are so many details and decisions to make. Should I add earrings? Would she want to wear that necklace I bought her for our anniversary? Do we want programs, a guest book, a graveside service? It all overwhelms me, but by Monday evening, everything seems to be ready for Friday's service. After dinner, I put Jessica to bed, and Colin and I sit together in front of the TV, watching an episode of *JAG*. This quickly becomes our nighttime routine, offering a sense of stability.

On Wednesday, our pastor, along with my parents, Charmaine's parents, and my brother and sister-in-law, come to the house to go over the details of the service. I tell the pastor about my conversation with Colin, and we decide to title the pastor's message "Mommy Is with Jesus."

I miss Charmaine like crazy, and it's comforting to have Pastor there. But I'm not despondent. I really do believe she's with Jesus in heaven.

After everyone leaves, Colin and I eat dinner, and then I feed Jessica and settle her in for the night. Colin and I sit down to watch *JAG*. By now, there is no question about where Colin will sleep. We are both comforted by being together, and each time I wake up during the night, it's comforting not to be alone.

The day of the funeral, I wake up early. It is still dark outside, and Colin is still asleep beside me. Jessica is sound asleep in her crib. I haven't slept much, and I go over the day in my mind, like reviewing a checklist of tasks. I will be driving Charmaine's parents to the cemetery and afterward to the church. My brother and sister-in-law are having everyone over to their home following the service.

When my thoughts are disrupted by Jessica's crying, I rise quietly so Colin will continue sleeping. After feeding and changing Jessica, we head downstairs to get ready for the day.

Only a few family members and close friends attend the graveside service, and then we head to the church for the main service. There are many friends and coworkers of Charmaine's, as well as our friends and our family. The praise band from church sings, and my heart hurts looking at the empty spot where she normally stood. I am so grateful to everyone who attends, but I'm kind of a private person, so it's hard to be the center of attention, and I'm glad when the service is over. It's clear that Charmaine was well loved and will be missed.

At the end of the day, as Colin and I settle in to watch *JAG*, I am completely exhausted—but not so tired that the pain doesn't hurt my heart.

When I wake Saturday morning, I make some coffee and sit in the living room trying to make sense of my life. I cannot believe Charmaine is gone, and I cannot believe I am now on my own with Colin and Jessica.

It doesn't seem that long ago that Charmaine and I were dating. She and I met while moonlight bowling, when I'd been assigned the same lane as her. Joyful and fun, she was a much-needed breath of fresh air in my life. I was getting over a difficult relationship, so we took things slow.

In 1995, we had been dating for over a year when we had a conversation that almost cost me our relationship.

We had just finished dinner at my house, and the conversation turned to future plans.

"How many children do you want to have?" she asked.

"I'm not sure I want children."

She paused while looking at me with sad eyes. "I'm so sorry, but I can't date you anymore."

As I watched her gather her things to leave, my head spun. *What just happened?* I followed her to her car. "Can we talk about this?"

"There's really nothing to talk about. I want children and you don't," she said in a sad voice.

Just like that, she was gone. Fifteen minutes later, I called her and asked if we could meet and talk.

The following evening over dinner, I shared my fears about having children. "I'm not sure I would make a good dad," I told her. "I'm the youngest child in my family, so I never helped care for younger siblings. And I haven't spent a lot of time around kids."

"I think you'll be a great dad." Then she added, "And besides, we'll be doing this together. You won't be raising them on your own."

She was right. I love being a dad. The last four years with Colin have been the happiest years of my life. I had been looking forward to our new family time together once Jessica was a little older and we could do more. I wish Charmaine had been right about us "doing this together." But the reality of it is setting in, and I am not afraid. I have peace. Since God has allowed me to be a single dad, I know He will get me through life. Somehow.

I take another sip of coffee before hearing Colin coming down the stairs and then the sound of Jessica crying in her crib. I grab a bottle to heat for Jessica and a bowl for Colin's cereal. After I feed and change Jessica, the three of us sit on the couch together to watch a few kids' shows. One program leads to another, and it's nice to sit still and not have to plan anything.

Later, while I'm doing laundry, the phone rings. It's Lynn, the owner of Colin's day care.

"You're going to need help with Colin and Jessica," she says. "So I've decided to postpone my retirement for a year."

She is also organizing dinners to be provided for us. The other day care families will take turns bringing dinner to the day care so I can take it with us when I pick up Colin and Jessica in the afternoon. Although I know the road ahead will be difficult, it is also one with lots of support. My parents and Charmaine's parents are available to help with Colin and Jessica's care, and now I have Lynn's day care available for another year.

I thank her over and over before hanging up the phone.

When Monday morning hits, I discover that getting the three of us ready in the morning is no small feat.

Jessica's not awake yet, and I don't want to wake her, but I have to. I pick her up as Colin slides into the room.

"Dad, don't wake her up. She'll start crying. Mommy never wakes her up."

"I have to wake her, Colin. I have to get you guys to day care." I lay Jessica on the changing table.

Colin hands me a diaper from the cloth stacker. "She's getting ready to cry, Dad. I can see it. She's gonna cry."

Jessica lets out a wail. Colin covers his ears and runs out.

"Colin, go get those clothes I laid out for you last night," I yell as Jessica cries harder.

By 8:00 a.m., I manage to have them dressed and in the car. I know if Charmaine had been here, it would have gone smoother. Then I remember that if Charmaine were still here, the kids would have stayed home with her. Deep sadness engulfs me as I buckle Jessica into her car seat.

After Colin and Jessica are settled in at the day care, I stop by the cemetery.

Unlike the last time I stood at my wife's grave, on the day of the funeral, I am no longer in shock. I somehow did not completely grasp the idea that the service was for my wife. It felt more like attending the funeral of someone I didn't know that well.

Now, as I'm standing here alone, it's very real.

The cemetery is silent. The only sound is a plane passing overhead. I stay for a long time just looking at the flowers and the temporary headstone. I hear cars come and go, but I just stand there. I like the quiet, and I feel calm now. I need to go to work, but I cannot make my feet move.

I just cannot believe my thirty-six-year-old wife is gone from this earth forever.

CHAPTER 8

Will He Ever Wake Up?

NANCY

The next morning, just before dawn, I swing the car into my usual parking spot and grab my water bottle from the center console. I am encouraged that my husband is alive and that the brain swelling continues to decrease—and this morning they will remove his breathing tube. I am grateful his infection appears to be resolving. He responded quickly to the new antibiotic, so his fever went down last night.

I pass through the empty waiting room and push the button to open the ICU doors. When the nurse looks up, I give her a wave and enter my husband's room. Everything is as it has been for the last ten days. I have grown accustomed to the beeping of machines and the eerie stillness. I sit by his bed while nurses draw blood, suction his mouth, and check the monitors.

I cannot believe that less than two weeks ago, our lives were normal. Just before the surgery, Keith had been away on a business trip in Taiwan. We talked every night by phone. I'd hold the phone up so the kids could hear him say, "I love you, and I will see you soon." Now, he's unable to move or speak. He looks so thin after only a week and a half.

I try hard to stay focused on the good news of the day—the removal of his breathing tube. And I try not to think about the future. One day at a time.

A morning update from his nurse interrupts my thoughts. The doctor will be in soon to extubate him so he can begin to breathe on his own. I'm hopeful that this will be a big step in the right direction and what is needed to wake him up. I imagine him waking up and being able to speak. I imagine him asking questions as he tries to figure out what happened and why he's still in the hospital.

Shortly after 9:00 a.m., the doctor and several nurses come in to remove the tube. I step out into the waiting room. They've told me the process could take some time, so I settle in to wait. I've just started to check phone messages and make notes about calls I need to return when I notice his nurse heading toward me. Sitting forward, I cannot believe how quickly they have not only removed the tube but have him ready for me to see him.

But I should know by now that things aren't right by the look on the nurse's face.

When they extubated him, his throat quickly closed, making it impossible for him to breathe. They had to intubate him again right away. She tells me she'll come get me when it's okay for me to see him. Discouraged, I sink back into my chair. Will he ever be able to breathe on his own?

After ten more minutes, I'm allowed into his room. He looks exactly as he did earlier—a tube through his mouth helping him to breathe. The doctor explains that due to the extent of the damage to my husband's throat during the surgery, there is too much swelling. The best option to allow him to breathe on his own is a surgical procedure called a tracheostomy. Though he describes the procedure as "relatively simple," panic rises in my own throat. Just a week and a half ago, we'd arrived at the hospital for a "simple outpatient surgery." I can't consider any surgery simple now. I focus on taking deep breaths as I ask questions.

Although my husband does not have a bleeding disorder, I keep thinking, what if he does now? What if this surgery is the final straw—the one that kills him in his weakened state? I am so conflicted. If he doesn't have this procedure, he cannot breathe on his own, but what if there are more complications? I remind myself that this is a different surgeon, a surgeon well respected by the nurses. I talk myself through the odds of something else happening.

But all my reasoning and pep talks do little to help me. I kind of wish the hospital chaplain were here to pray about this surgery. Nonetheless, seeing Keith progress is my top priority, so I decide to move forward.

When they wheel him out of ICU toward the elevators, I'm truly scared. Maybe I should have known something bad could happen with the first surgery. What if he does die in this surgery—I really will be the one to blame.

Once he's in surgery, fear bubbles up in my stomach. I choose a chair near the door of the OR waiting room in case I need to make a quick escape. As I wait, I replay the last week and half in my head. I consider praying, but without the chaplain, I really don't know how. The prayers I know are from the Catholic background I'd grown up in—memorized prayers for the sole purpose of hopefully getting into heaven. As a child, I tried so hard to be perfect and follow the rules . . . and wound up with lots of guilt, which led me to quit praying altogether.

Within fifteen minutes, the surgeon is standing in front of me with a good report. The trach is in, and my husband is breathing.

I jump out of my chair and hug the surgeon. "Thank you!"

The next afternoon, I go out to grab a cup of coffee, and my husband is awake when I return to his room. It is not quite as eventful as I'd imagined it would be. He's groggy and unaware of where he is, and he shows little interest in figuring it out.

I pull the chair closer to the bed and lean in close to him. I lay a hand on his cheek. "You are okay," I whisper.

He looks dazed and confused but seems to know who I am. What a relief.

He falls asleep and wakes up several times. The nurses ask him questions each time he wakes up, but he can't answer. Although he moves his lips as if answering, no sound comes out. I lean in close again, hoping to hear him, but no whisper drifts to my ears.

After a few minutes of this, I step into the hallway with his nurse, and she explains that the X-rays show that his vocal cords were damaged during the surgery. With time, they should recover. She also tells me that since he will not be able to swallow food properly, they will also need to place a feeding tube in him. The tube will allow him to have liquid nutrition administered directly into his stomach.

Next, the speech therapist comes in with a laminated strip of simple pictures my husband can point to. I am familiar with these pictures. They are the same method of communication we've used with Billy since his autism diagnosis.

"Who are you?" the therapist asks.

My husband points to a picture of a dog.

When the therapist asks him to point to a picture of a dog, my husband points to the car instead.

Oh no, this is just great. Now there are three people in our family with limited communication skills. I quickly give myself a pep talk. This will be okay. He's just survived a horrible ordeal, so why is it important for him to be able to point to a picture of a dog?

Later in the afternoon, the physical therapist comes in to assess him. Although Keith seems to have good mobility on his left side, the right side of his body is completely paralyzed. His physical therapist assures me this is not necessarily a permanent state and encourages me to give it time.

The stroke has caused significant damage, and Keith also has trouble making himself understood. He has virtually no sound, since his vocal cords have been damaged, plus he has a trach, which causes him to whisper in a Darth Vader voice. It's difficult to figure out what he means, especially because he thinks I should be able to understand him—all of which leaves him continually frustrated.

I try having him write out his thoughts, but what he hands me are a bunch of random letters. They make sense to him. That makes one of us.

One evening, I show up with more pictures of the kids and picture frames. Although I had hoped to get the pictures in the frames while I was home, it hadn't happened. Either Billy or Riley or sometimes both of them were in my lap most of the afternoon. So I proceed to put the pictures in the frames while I'm in Keith's room.

I set a picture of Billy and Keith on a shelf near Keith's bed. He keeps pointing at it and whispering something I can't make out.

I ask him to say it again. He does, and I'm still at a loss.

I pick up the frame and hand it to him. "It's you and Billy. I thought you might want it here."

He shakes his head, points to Billy in the picture, and again says something that makes no sense.

I can tell he's getting frustrated.

"Oh, I know what you want," I say. "You want this picture in the frame." I pick up the paper picture that was in the frame when I bought it and wave it in front of him.

He shakes his head now and silently laughs.

I quickly move to a different topic, and the distraction works.

That night as I make the drive home, I am grateful my husband is awake, but for the first time, things sink in. As a former special education teacher, I'm able to visualize the road ahead. This may be a long recovery. I replay conversations with his doctor and therapists: "He is young"; "He was healthy before the stroke"; "He has a good chance at recovery"; "It just takes time."

When I return the next morning, the update is all good news. He is more alert, his labs show his infection has completely cleared up, and from a medical standpoint, he is stable enough to begin preparing for a move to a rehabilitation hospital.

Though we cannot have conversation, I hold his hand. With my other hand, I brush the hair from his forehead and whisper to him about how amazing Billy and Riley are and how much they love and miss him. I show him family pictures and tell him stories.

Is any of this getting through to him?

CHAPTER 9

Rehab Realities

NANCY

When the doorbell dings early the next morning, I jump up from my chair in the kitchen, coffee still in hand, and race to answer it. It's Tiffini, arms laden with construction paper, fake flowers, and tape. She's arrived to teach the preschool we hold at our house—regular preschool is too overwhelming for Billy, so a few neighborhood kids gather at our house.

The other students are typical (not disabled) three- and four-year-olds. They model play skills and speech for Billy.

Since Billy's diagnosis with autism, I have become familiar with speech therapy, ABA (applied behavioral analysis) therapy, and occupational therapy to help him with his sensory issues. In fact, for over a year now, Billy has had therapy five days a week.

Even though I am familiar with these therapy sessions, nothing could have prepared me for selecting a rehabilitation facility for my husband. With Tiffini taking charge of the preschool class, Beth and I are free to begin this daunting process.

As I tour the local facilities, I have so much to consider. It isn't just the quality of the program but also the nursing staff and the ages of the other patients. Most of the people recovering from strokes are much older than my thirty-eight-year-old husband. The younger patients are receiving rehabilitation for traumatic brain injuries. When Beth and I tour that area, it's loud and chaotic.

Beth and I narrow the choices based on the size of the rehabilitation gym and the upbeat energy of the staff, which suggests that the facility is less of a nursing home and more focused on recovery. When one of our top choices offers a room with two beds, the decision is easy. It is highly appealing to have my own bed to sleep in at night.

Three days later, as we prepare to leave the ICU by ambulance for the rehab hospital, I hear a familiar voice. It takes me a minute to place the voice, but then I realize it's the anonymous caller from several weeks ago.

I turn. Several nurses are sitting at the nurses' station—one man among them.

I look specifically at the nurse who was both brave and kind enough to make that call to me, and I say, "Thank you."

"You're welcome," he replies.

"No, really, thank you for everything," I emphasize.

"Got it." He gives me a smile.

As I follow the ambulance and pull into the parking lot of the rehabilitation hospital, I'm both excited and nervous. I know we will miss the intense nursing care in the ICU, but I'm also hopeful that this will be the place where my husband will fully recover.

I have prepared his new room as much as possible. Even though it has pink curtains, I am sure the kids' pictures and some motivational posters on the wall will make it more appealing. In addition to the small TV above his bed, I have purchased a TV with a built-in VCR and stocked his nightstand with his favorite action movies.

After I place his clothes and shoes in the closet, a nurse arrives to give him some medications and "food"—liquid that is poured directly into his stomach through his feeding tube.

Unfortunately, just as quickly as the food goes in, it comes out. His stomach cannot handle much, and the nurses decide to feed him slowly, using a feeding pump instead. His liquid food is poured into an IV bag and connected to his feeding tube. This will allow him to "eat" over the course of several hours.

As we settle in for the night, everything seems calm and quiet. There are no monitors beeping, and except for the occasional phone call coming in to the nurses' desk, the only sound I hear is the ticking of the clock on the wall.

I fall asleep but am awakened less than an hour later by my husband's cough. Unlike in the ICU, no one rushes in to help him. I hit the call button.

"May I help you?" someone says through the speaker on the wall.

"Yes, my husband is coughing," I respond.

"Okay, I'll page respiratory therapy."

A few minutes later, the respiratory therapist arrives to help my husband cough stuff out of his trach so he can sleep again. Less than two hours later, we repeat the same process. After the fourth episode, I realize this is the new norm for us.

Our first morning at the rehab center is a rude awakening. We have gone from the ICU, where the focus is survival and pain management, to an 8:00 a.m. physical therapy session. The nurse arrives at 7:30 to help my husband with the clothing I have selected.

I watch as my husband, who used to wear a suit and tie, now receives help pulling on elastic-waist shorts and a T-shirt. The nurse helps but also requires that he do all he can.

It's hard to watch him struggle. I want to jump in and help when he cannot find the openings in the T-shirt for his head and arms.

"Nancy, please just stay in the chair." She motions for me to sit back down. "Keith needs to do as much as he can on his own, to build up his skills."

She kneels and shows him some tricks for getting his shoes on with the use of only one hand, and then he successfully secures the Velcro straps.

Two physical therapists, one on each side, assist him in the transfer from the bed to a wheelchair and push him down the hall to the gym. Although nervous about his limitations, I feel hopeful when I see him stand with support. With a belt around his waist and a therapist on each side, he is able to put weight on his legs, and he remains in a standing position by holding on to a walker for support. After physical therapy, we stay in the gym for occupational therapy. He is wheeled over to a table where he will place each hand on a pedal, and then by turning the pedals, a wheel will turn. It is kind of like riding a bike, only your hands do the work.

This activity doesn't go as well.

Although he has no trouble using his left hand to move the pedal, his right hand repeatedly falls from the pedal and hits the table with a thud.

Over and over, the occupational therapist encourages him in a gentle voice. "Try it again."

He doesn't master it that day, but he never gives up either.

Speech therapy is next, and although not physical, it turns out to be the most exhausting. Since he has made few sounds because of the damage to his vocal cords, the therapist encourages him to produce vocal words while she also reads his lips. He sounds like an elderly heavy smoker. His voice, coming through his trach, is raspy. Each time he tries to speak, it's followed by a coughing spell.

Although I catch on quickly with lip reading, the speech therapist is much better than I am. One of our biggest problems is that he often mouths entirely different words than he thinks he is. The speech therapist talks about apraxia (inability to produce intended action because of brain damage) and aphasia (inability to express or understand speech because of brain damage). Both are parts of the struggle with stroke recovery.

I know what she's talking about. One of the ways I have made him laugh in the past few days is by guessing what he is saying and responding with something ridiculous and funny. Humor helps decrease the frustration for both of us.

After an hour and a half of therapies, my husband needs a nap. As I help him remove his shoes and cover him with a blanket, I am struck by a thought. This is the same person who used to travel internationally and walk directly into meetings with no sleep and serious jet lag. Now, after being awake for a couple of hours, he needs a nap.

He falls into a deep sleep within a matter of minutes. I gather my things, ask the nurse to please listen for his coughing, and head for the parking lot. It's only 10:00 a.m.

Thirty minutes later, I walk into the house and am greeted with the sounds of happy kids. Although I'm overwhelmed with what we're facing, I am so grateful that my mom and Diane are keeping the kids happy and fed.

Riley is in her high chair, neatly picking up pieces of cubed vegetables, and she laughs when she sees me. I hear Tiffini's cheerful voice coming from downstairs and realize Billy is in his session with her. I hear the familiar words "Your turn" followed by "Great job, Billy." I am reminded again of all the things that come naturally to Riley that Billy has to be taught over and over.

I grab a cup of coffee as I sit down to make a list of everything I need to do before I return to the hospital. While I update my mom on the rehab hospital, I hear Billy's little feet coming up the stairs. When he sees me, he runs at full speed, then jumps into my lap, saying "Mmmmmm," which is his word for Mommy or sometimes milk. But this time he is saying Mommy.

While Riley naps, Billy and I sit on the couch and watch a *Barney* episode. During his favorite parts, he runs up to the TV and stands there, smiling. Then he returns to the couch, climbs up, and settles his head against my arm. I doze off a couple of times but wake up as he launches from the couch to get a close-up view of another favorite scene.

After dinner and bath time, my mom and I put the kids in the double stroller and take a walk around the neighborhood. This is the calmest and most normal thing I have done in ages. I make a mental note that we should do this every evening. It's nice to see some neighborhood life, people mowing lawns, and kids riding bikes. We used to be like this.

I try to imagine us being like this again, but in reality, I'm not so sure.

CHAPTER 10

Nurse Nancy

NANCY

One Sunday afternoon when I go to visit my husband, there is a beautifully wrapped present on his nightstand. He eagerly motions that it's for me. When I open the card, I realize it is Mother's Day. I had forgotten. If my mom hadn't had to return home, her presence might have reminded me. But we are so focused on the daily therapies and my husband's health that our regular life has faded away.

I tear open the gift wrap and am surprised to see a large, framed picture of Billy and Riley sitting in a wagon with cute outfits on and the best smiles on their faces. Another features them sitting in a huge crayon box.

I wipe away tears and wonder how my husband could have accomplished this.

Wait. Of course, he didn't.

Tiffini!

When I ask her later, she tells me how she sang and danced her heart out getting Billy to smile while the professional photographer just kept snapping away. Anyone who has a child with autism knows how difficult getting a good picture can be, and I feel incredibly blessed by friends and family who continue to stand beside us during this difficult time.

We are now in our fifth week at the rehab hospital and have the routine down. The mornings are therapy sessions (physical, occupational, and speech) followed by a nap—which is when I go home to be with the kids. In the afternoon, my husband endures another round of therapy before dinnertime. Unfortunately, dinner continues to be liquid through his feeding tube.

In the evenings after my neighborhood walk with the kids, I return to the hospital for the night. After the update from the nurse, I settle into my bed. My husband and I sync our individual televisions to the same channel and watch a rerun of *Seinfeld* or another comedy. During the funny parts, I glance over at him to see his body shaking with laughter. Although he still has little sound, seeing him laugh warms my heart.

After we watch a couple of shows, the nurse brings his sleeping medication, and within minutes he is out.

Sleep is not so easy for me. I try to will myself to sleep because I know within a short amount of time the coughing will start.

While I'm not required to be there overnight, I know that if Keith wakes up coughing, he might not be able to find the call button. Even if he does, he will not be heard very well, due to his raspy voice. That's not a chance I want to take, so I sacrifice my own sleep for his sake.

My husband is making great progress in some areas, but in others he is at a standstill. In physical therapy, he often receives cheers from the staff and other patients as he does laps around the gym using his cane. I am grateful for his quick progress from a walker to a quad cane to a regular cane. Although a therapist still walks beside him, he no longer needs someone holding on to his therapy belt.

He has also made progress in occupational therapy. With enough focus, he can use his right hand to stack small blocks. In another activity, he uses a wooden board with holes in it. He is able to hold the end of a shoelace and weave it through the board. He can also hold something in his right hand and not drop it, as long as his entire focus is on the item. When we first arrived, he was unable to do any of these activities.

With his speech, there is not much progress. He can repeat things, and his sound quality has improved some, making it easier to hear what he is trying to say. I am concerned, however, with his lack of retention. We work on the same things day after day after day. He cannot articulate his address or even what city he lives in. When asked, he offers only a blank stare, as if he's being asked for the first time.

Even choosing the correct answer from a list of options is difficult for him. When the therapist asks him to point to something he would eat, the options are bed, chair, pizza, and ball. Keith would read through the options and point to one—usually the wrong one.

Hard to make a joke about his eating a chair.

A couple of weeks later, the speech therapist says to me, "I have some exciting news."

It's been a while since I've been in a session with them. I knew they were working on Keith learning his address. When they started, the speech therapist would read his address from a piece of paper that Keith could follow along with.

"He has progressed to the point that he can now say his address from memory," the therapist adds.

Keith grins from ear to ear, ready to whisper our address to me.

I sit down and wait. Keith gathers his thoughts, looks at me, and slowly says an address.

"Wow, Keith, that's great!" I cheer him on and rub his shoulder.

As we leave the room, Keith is ahead of me, so I turn to the therapist. "You know that he didn't get it correct, right?"

She looks surprised and shows me the printed address she had taught him from. The numbers had been transposed! He had worked for three weeks to memorize the wrong address.

Great. That is just great.

One of the things I look forward to most is the Sunday visits from Pastor Ben, a tall, bearded man. On this Sunday, he walks into our room and stands by my husband's bed. Since it's the weekend, Keith is still in bed relaxing and gearing up for his week of therapy.

After I give the pastor a quick update, he prays for us.

"Father, we thank You for Keith's recovery so far. We ask for continued healing and blessings on Keith and his family."

As he prays, he holds his hands over Keith's body, especially his throat area. Though I never share all the details with him, Pastor Ben always seems to know what's going on.

I am amazed for two reasons. First, with the exception of the hospital chaplain, I have never heard anyone pray like this. I am used to rote prayers, memorized prayers, prayers that are prayed more out of duty than the expectation of them being answered.

Second, I am amazed that the things the pastor prays for are often answered the following week. One time, he prayed for Keith to gain more mobility, and two days later, Keith was able to move his leg in a more normal way, without it swinging out the side with each step.

I start to realize that prayer is really simply talking with God. There doesn't have to be an emergency situation to pray, and you can speak as if you're just talking with a friend. Still, I never pray on my own. I guess I don't believe I am qualified, and I know from my failure to keep the Ten Commandments, I am not deserving of God's time.

One night as my husband and I are preparing for our evening TV time, a nurse walks in.

"Hey, Keith. Here are your nighttime meds." She puts them into his feeding tube. "Do you need anything?" She checks his pulse. "I bet you can't wait to go home. It will probably only be a few more days."

My eyes bulge. "You mean . . . once the feeding tube and trach are out."

"Well." She smiles in a way that I'm sure is meant to be encouraging. "Many patients go home with them and do just fine."

She leaves then, and I find it hard to breathe.

A few minutes later, my husband peacefully drifts off to sleep, no doubt excited about thoughts of going home. I toss and turn all night, trying to imagine how in the world I can provide the care the nurses and respiratory therapists provide.

The next morning, I track the respiratory therapist down, and spill out what the nurse had said.

"Oh, don't worry." She touches my arm in a reassuring way, which gives me a brief sense of relief, knowing she understands my fear. "I'll teach you how to do everything before you leave."

Her words do little to reassure me. At the rehab hospital, there is a day and night shift of respiratory therapists. How can I possibly do their jobs around the clock?

Before I can properly process this and our possible new reality, Keith's nurses and therapists commence chattering about how great it will be for him to be in familiar surroundings and home with his kids.

I seem to be the only one who doesn't get it. All I can think about is how *alone* we'll be.

Once I get to the point of being a bit more clearheaded, I contact our insurance company. Surely, there has to be a better alternative than for me to become Nurse Nancy. To my dismay, they present two options: They will either cover some nursing care at home or outpatient occupational, physical, and speech therapy. Since I know I cannot do the therapies, I opt to be his nurse. But believe me, if we had the money, I would hire a live-in nurse in a heartbeat.

As promised, our last week in the rehab hospital is training for me. I am summoned to his bedside every time a nurse or respiratory therapist comes in to perform a procedure. Twice a day I must clean his feeding tube and the area near the skin by wiping both with a cotton swab and alcohol to keep it from getting infected. If the tube becomes clogged, I must syringe water into it and work the clog loose. They teach me how to run the feeding pump and how to resolve things when the pump malfunctions or the end connecting to his body comes loose.

The respiratory therapist teaches me the process of "coughing him." First, glove up, then, since he cannot breathe because of the mucus in his lungs, quickly twist the outer latch of the trach and remove the inner cannula by pulling it straight out while at the same time covering the opening with a cloth so the mucus doesn't shoot out all over us. Then spray a little saline into the hole to help him cough more. Be sure to get the cloth back in place quickly after spraying the saline. Repeat this over and over until he is done coughing. Then clean the inner cannula, put it back in him, and secure it with the latch.

This needs to be done quickly so he can breathe again, and since he is coughing and moving, it's difficult. The good news is, I receive plenty of practice, since this is done both day and night every few hours. The bad news is, it's exhausting, and trying to calm down and sleep after the adrenaline rush is challenging.

Two days before his discharge date, I sit down with a nurse to make a chart for his medications.

Some are given every two hours, others every four, and some just once a day. If the medication doesn't come in liquid form, it must be crushed, mixed in water, placed in a syringe, and administered through his feeding tube.

"Thank you for helping me, Susan." Overwhelmed, I yawn, then cover my mouth with my hand. "I'm wondering which of these are liquid and which are tablets. And how do you crush the tablets to make them small enough to fit through his feeding tube?"

Susan pats my arm. "You're going to be fine. You can buy a pill grinder to crush the tablets. Just crush them into the finest powder you can. Then mix it right in with the liquid medications. Pour them into a measuring cup or something that has a spout so you won't spill it when you put it into the tube. Let's go into Keith's room now so I can show you what to do if the tube gets clogged."

I follow her to Keith's room, thinking, *Okay, you can do this . . . you can do this.*

The next day, while I'm home snuggling on the couch with Billy for our afternoon *Barney* video, the doorbell rings. The medical supply company delivers the hospital bed, a wheelchair (for long-distance outings), a bedside toilet, a feeding pump, IV bags, trach supplies, and many boxes of liquid nutrition.

Our main bedroom instantly resembles a hospital room.

CHAPTER 11

Home Sweet Home—Not

NANCY

A raspy whisper wakes me up in the middle of the night. "Hey . . . hey
. . . the feeding tube is leaking."

Not again. I am so tired. Despite my exhaustion, I roll out of my
bed and help my husband to a chair in our bedroom. I then repair the
feeding tube, change all his bedding, and restart the IV feeding. Once
I settle him back into bed, I hope I'll fall asleep as quickly as he does.

But sleep eludes me, and along with the exhaustion, anger sets in.

I'd begun this new adventure in our lives by trying to establish
a routine. But getting cooperation from a toddler, a three-year-old
with autism, and a husband recovering from a brain injury is nearly
impossible. Surprisingly, the person with the least amount of patience
is my husband.

He has a hard time with even the simplest of tasks, and since he
was someone who could do most anything prior to his stroke, the fact
that he can't see the hairbrush that is right in front of him drives him
to distraction.

And it means he needs my help. He will call me in that raspy voice
or come stand in the hallway while I'm fixing lunch for the kids. If
he needs or wants something, he expects me to be right there. I know
he's frustrated, but I'm pulled pretty thin with the kids' needs and his.

Fortunately, during the daytime hours, his coughing episodes
happen less often. The nights are still difficult since he needs to be

coughed every couple of hours. I have become such a light sleeper that I wake up every time he moves. I imagine what it must be like for him to be completely reliant on someone else to help him breathe.

In addition to the coughing, I also wake to my name being called—at least once a week, which is more often than I'd like—in that raspy voice, letting me know that the feeding tube is leaking.

The disrupted sleep and the early mornings with the kids take a toll. Before preschool every day, I'd long ago established a time for reading and interacting with Billy and Riley. After Keith came home, we kept the preschool going in order to maintain Billy's routine. Silly me—I think if I just keep all the plates spinning, things will work out.

Even with Diane's help with the kids, this new mixture of exhaustion and anger depletes my energy even further. My only break comes when I drive my husband to outpatient therapy three times a week. During the two and a half hours he is there, I run errands and return phone calls without interruption.

A couple times a week, I can also count on Beth to come by in her red truck. When Billy hears her truck, he runs to the living room sofa and peers through the window as she parks on the street. He jumps up and down, making a happy squealing noise. I add the words to go with his emotions. Since he doesn't have the words yet, we help him by saying them for him. "Oh, you are so happy" and "You love riding in the big red truck."

"I'm here to take my favorite three-year-old for a drive!" Beth says when she enters the house. We talk, or try to talk, for a few minutes, but Billy has hold of her hand, and he is doing all he can to pull her to the door.

"Thanks so much, Beth," I say as Billy yanks her out the door and up the steps. I put Riley in her playpen and catch up to them to help with the car seat.

Billy stands on the sidewalk jumping up and down. He can barely contain his excitement. He loves her truck! Beth straps his car seat in, and the two of them take off for a fifteen-minute drive.

Because Billy is sensitive to loud noises, I use this time to vacuum, while Diane takes a break and grabs a cup of coffee.

Diane and I both feel the strain of the day-to-day juggle, though somehow, we manage.

When Diane asks for a few days off to get out of town, I'm not sure what to do. She deserves it, and this is clearly not the job we hired her for, but how will I manage without her? I call my mom, and she agrees to hop on a plane to come help.

My mom and I manage well during Diane's absence, but it's difficult at times because I must teach Mom some of our routine, which slows down the process. I know I am blessed to have Diane and can't wait for her to return.

When the phone rings one night, I assume it's Beth, letting me know when she'll come to pick up Billy tomorrow.

I'm wrong. It's Diane.

"How is your trip going, Diane?"

"It's good, but that's not why I'm calling."

Uh-oh.

"Is something wrong?" Maybe she isn't going to return on time. I may have to ask my mom to stay longer. Then she says the words I am not ready to hear.

"I'm really sorry, Nancy. I've loved working with you and the kids, but it's just so much more than I signed up for. I'm not able to keep doing it."

I feel numb but manage to say, "I understand. I really do. When will you be back, and how long can you stay?"

"I will come by next week to get my stuff, but I cannot return to the job. I am so sorry."

Reeling, I plop into an armchair near the phone. "You mean, ever? If you just need more time off—"

"No, Nancy. I'm resigning. I'm not coming back. I'll be by in a couple days to pack up my stuff."

Although she has told me twice that she's leaving, I still can't believe it because I don't want to believe it. What am I going to do?

I hang up in a daze but don't have time to process, as my mom is calling me from the kitchen to help her with the oven. The previous owners put in a top-of-the-line oven. Apparently, it can do every single thing you want, but it complicates the simple cooking we want to do. I wander to the kitchen and push all the stupid buttons. *Stupid oven. Stupid, stupid oven.* Even as I'm thinking that, I know my frustration is not with the oven.

That night after everyone is in bed, I start talking to God. I go into the garage, where no one will hear me, and yell, "Really, God! How? How am I supposed to do this?" I open the car door and slide into the front seat. I close the door, and with tears streaming down my face, I pound the steering wheel and yell. I cannot even form words—I alternate between yelling at the top of my lungs and sobbing. I lean against the steering wheel, gripping it as tight as I can. I need to pull it together for the people inside, the people who are expecting me to solve every problem, the people who expect me to keep it together since they can't.

Afterward, I feel awful about yelling at God, but I'm still not sure how in the world I will manage when my mom goes home.

The next day at a follow-up appointment with the ENT, the doctor says it's time to remove the trach. He is confident that breathing will no longer be a problem, but he makes it clear that eating is still out of the question since Keith has so much trouble swallowing. The doctor suggests therapy to work on proper swallowing so my husband will not aspirate food into his airway.

The nights will go smoother without the trach care, and I lower my tensed shoulders in relief.

Since he's been home, Keith has come down with aspiration pneumonia five times. Fever. Lethargy. Heavy-duty antibiotics. Stomach issues and throwing up, which prevents healing. Each time, he has lost ground in occupational therapy and physical therapy.

Without the trach, he will be less likely to aspirate. We are heading in the right direction.

But financially, we still have some decisions to make. We have great insurance, but as Keith is now on disability, we're living on half our normal income. Although I have not talked to Keith about our finances, I know I need to get our house on the market as soon as possible. My plan is to list it for sale as soon as we are able to return all the hospital equipment and make our main bedroom presentable enough to show the house.

A few weeks later, after my mom leaves, my friend Anne—Will's wife—comes to help for two weeks. She not only pitches in anytime she's needed, she also has this energy about her that lets me know things will be okay. She is fun and silly, and we often laugh hysterically over really dumb things. Billy and Riley love her because of her willingness to sing and dance along with whatever children's video they are watching.

One day she and I want to get some exercise besides the neighborhood walk with the kids, so we decide to work out to the kids show *Veggie Tales*. That way Billy and Riley are entertained, and we get a workout. The songs are energetic. We roll out our yoga mats on the floor in front of the TV and start dancing to the song "Tall Silk Hat." It isn't too long before we are both laughing so hard that we are on the ground with tears rolling down our faces. It feels really good to laugh this hard.

On her last night in town, she tells me what she knows about God and shares Bible verses with me. It's as if she's speaking a foreign language. I want to understand, but I just don't. I do not own a Bible—I have never even opened a Bible.

After she leaves, I am on my own. Laundry piles up. Dishes stack on the counter. Mail overflows on the hallway table. I manage only feeding, bathing, and getting everyone to bed. Plus, I make sure to read and play with the kids—which helps me shove the piles to the back of my mind.

I know I need to make a call to the nanny agency to try to find us some help.

The thing is, I have no idea how to explain the job. I mean, really, who would want this job? Finally, I make the call.

"Hi, I would like to put in a request for a nanny. You helped us before, with Diane Smith, but as you know, she left last month."

"Okay . . ." I can hear the concern in the woman's voice. "Tell me a little more about what you are looking for."

"Well, I'm not sure we want a live-in person, but I'm also open to that if it's the right person."

"What are the hours you are looking for?"

"We're flexible on the hours—we just need help!"

"I see."

She wants to set hours, but I just want help, and I do not want to limit our options by having set hours. She finally gives up on setting hours and says she will be in touch soon.

I hang up feeling very discouraged. Just the interview process alone seems overwhelming, not to mention what will happen when the reality of our situation becomes apparent to a potential nanny. Who would want this job?

The following day, the woman from the agency calls. She has someone she wants me to meet. Her name is Hilary. She does not want a live-in or a full-time position. But the agency woman says, "I just have a feeling you two should meet."

CHAPTER 12

Long QT Syndrome

JEFF

Two weeks after my wife's death, the autopsy results come back without a cause of death. Her heart and brain were fine, and she did not fall. The coroner cannot determine the cause. She suggests I look through Charmaine's medical records to see if anything jumps out.

The next few nights, I look through my wife's medical files. I find information about her allergies. I find the records of her pregnancies. Everything seems normal and non–life threatening. Then I run across a file with an EKG of my wife's heart and the term "long QT syndrome."

She never mentioned this to me, and I'm unfamiliar with it.

The following day, my mom shares a newspaper article about a woman—also Filipino and about Charmaine's age—who passed away shortly after having a baby. It turns out that long QT syndrome is a heart rhythm condition that can cause too long an interval between heartbeats. This can cause sudden fainting spells. In some cases, the heart can stop beating for so long that it causes sudden death.

I read a list of medications and supplements that can make long QT worse, and when I see antihistamines on the list, my heart sinks. Charmaine was taking antihistamines for her allergies.

I share this information with the coroner, and she decides that must be the cause of Charmaine's death. On the one hand, it's a relief to have at least a bit of closure, but on the other hand, I still wonder why this had to happen.

I spend the afternoon trying to focus on my work, but it seems like every few minutes I am wondering how we could have made sure she was okay. Are there specialists for long QT? Is there surgery to correct it? Could we have prevented her death? After many attempts to stay focused, I give up and leave work early.

On my way to pick up Colin and Jessica, I stop by the cemetery again. It has become part of my routine to stop in the morning and again in the afternoon. I know there will come a day when I will not stop to see her as much, but for now I need the calm and peace of that space.

I kneel by the gravestone. "I miss you so much, Charmaine. I promise I'll take good care of the kids." I know she cannot hear me, but it helps my grief to talk to her. "Everyone misses you."

I'm thankful for a few minutes of rest. At work, everyone is so sad every time they see me that I put in extra effort to be positive and upbeat while I'm there. It's exhausting.

I think about Charmaine's excitement when she found out we were having a girl. I think about the things we planned to do when the kids were a little older. I think about all the things she will miss—the Mother's Day parties at school, watching the kids open presents on Christmas, school plays, birthday parties, graduations, weddings. I wipe my tears with my sleeve and try not to break down. I have to stay strong for my kids.

Over the next few weeks, the gravesite visits decrease, and near the end of July, I decide I must make some changes. I've been focusing so much on her death and our loss, but I need to look ahead at what life will look like for this forty-three-year-old dad and his two young kids.

I talk with my brother about taking a smaller role in the company so I can make Jessica and Colin my first priority. Being an outside sales rep will give me flexibility and shorter hours.

Now I have two goals: make Charmaine proud of me as a dad and get through the next forty-five years.

One Saturday morning, I take Colin and Jessica to the wild animal park. Charmaine, Colin, and I had been there many times, and Colin is excited to see the animals again.

About ten minutes into our adventure at the park, I notice all the families—moms and dads with their kids and older couples walking hand in hand. I push the stroller as I listen to Colin tell Jessica all about each animal.

He leans into her stroller with an animated face before pointing to the monkey cages. "Look, Jessica! Aren't they cool!"

He mimes being a monkey, and Jessica squeals. He's such a great big brother, and it's fun to watch them together. Yet I'm sad that Charmaine isn't here to see this with us.

After two hours of hearing kids screaming, "Mommy, Mommy, look!" I need a break. I pack up the kids and our gear and head for home. I know I will get used to seeing complete happy families, but not today.

After dinner and baths, I settle into the rocking chair with Jessica, grateful that she sleeps through the night. As she drinks her bottle, I watch her little eyes droop. Once they're closed, I gently lay her in her crib.

I go downstairs to find Colin playing with his cars on the tile floor by the dining room. By now he knows the routine, so he puts them away, and we snuggle side by side on the couch for our nightly rerun of *JAG*. Afterward, we go upstairs and crawl into bed.

Tired, he insists I read *My Baseball Book* to him.

After I finish reading it, he says, "Dad, this is the book we bought with Mommy. Tell me *that* story."

Part of our nighttime routine now includes me telling him the story of buying the book. So I tell him again.

"When Mommy was getting ready to have your baby sister, she wanted to buy you a book about being a big brother. Mommy, Daddy, and Colin went to the bookstore. While we were there, you wanted to look at all the books, not just the books about being a big brother."

Colin interrupts me. "Dad, you forgot the part about stopping for ice cream first. You need to say that Mommy, Daddy, and Colin went to get ice cream and then went to the bookstore."

I start the story over and try to be sure I do not miss a single detail that is important to him. I do love thinking about that day. It was so perfect. Although Colin had no interest in the books on being a brother, he loved the books on sports, and now we have *My Baseball Book*, by Gail Gibbons, as a reminder of that day—a day when everything seemed right with the world.

CHAPTER 13

Derailed

NANCY

I arrange to meet Hilary while my husband is away at therapy and Billy is in his session with Tiffini. Riley can play quietly for a few minutes, at least long enough for me to tell Hilary about the job and then watch her run for the door.

I invite her to sit at the dining room table, and I take the chair closest to her.

"How long have you worked for the agency?" I ask.

"Only a short while this time. I did nanny jobs in the past but stopped for a bit to spend time with my four children." She tips her head. "I'd love to hear about your kids. What kind of help do you need with them?"

Ugh. I really don't want to tell her. Sure, she might be looking for a part-time nanny job, but not this. She's clearly very caring, but this is probably way more than she would ever want.

I explain our lives. She won't want the job, but I enjoy the fact that she really seems to care.

To my surprise, she doesn't run away, but says she would like to go home and talk to her husband.

The following day, she calls to ask if she can come over. Before we sit together at the table, I have prepared myself mentally for her to reject the job.

Instead, she looks at me with tears in her eyes. "I'm so glad you called me. I think I have a solution. I'd like to help, but I don't want to be paid."

I am speechless.

"I'm also wondering if you'd be willing to accept help from some of my friends from church. I can arrange rides for Keith to and from his therapy sessions so you can be home with the kids or just have a break."

The weight of the world lifts off me. I agree, and I again think that maybe God *is* listening.

The next day, my doorbell rings. I open it to two young women—Monica and Sharon. They are all smiles as they introduce themselves. Within a few hours, several other people show up, asking how they can help. Life suddenly feels manageable. Life feels better.

Monica and Sharon alternate days of driving Keith to and from his therapy appointments. Hilary and her children arrive most days to clean the kitchen and play with Billy and Riley. Another gal from Hilary's church, Val, likes to garden. Many days, I look out the window and see her planting flowers or pulling weeds. Val's husband is an electrician, so when the lights in the yard overheat, he shows up to handle it.

Along with having Beth, who gives Billy rides in the red truck twice a week, and our friend Mike and his dad, who so willingly show up with their tools every time I have a leak in the kitchen or some other plumbing issue, I now have a whole new set of friends to help us.

Could this be God working in my life—in my family's life? I want to believe it but can't quite imagine that He listens to regular people.

The only time I do not have help is on the weekends. But in an emergency, I have people I can call, and that makes all the difference. The problem with the weekends is that it is impossible for the four of us to get out of the house. Billy and Riley require the double stroller, and my husband needs the wheelchair for any distances.

One Sunday afternoon, our friend Debbie calls to suggest we go for a walk in the neighborhood. Debbie has two small children, so I cannot imagine how we can make this work. But she has it all planned out. She'll put her little one in a baby carrier. Her older son can walk, and she will push Billy and Riley in the double stroller. This will free me up to push the wheelchair. Although it sounds like a lot of work, it also sounds nice.

This feels normal, and I relax. Our friends truly are some of the best, and I feel like I can get through this with their help.

We get everything ready, including snacks for the kids, and begin our walk. We are having a conversation when suddenly, my husband's left arm shoots out at a weird angle and twitches rapidly. I set the brake and come around the side of the wheelchair. His whole body stiffens, and he shakes violently. I go back behind the wheelchair, loop my arms under his arms, and try to hold him in place so he will not fall to the ground. His whole body convulses while I hold on as tightly as I can.

"Call nine-one-one!" I yell.

Debbie pushes the double stroller just ahead of us—so my kids can't see their dad, I later realize—sets the brake, and grabs her phone. She dials and, while waiting for an answer, starts to run to the house we are standing in front of.

"A paramedic lives here!" she yells over her shoulder.

Before I know it, Debbie and a man—presumably the paramedic—run toward us.

"A doctor lives across the street," he tells Debbie, and she takes off running.

The paramedic and I lower Keith to the ground, and he starts working on him. The seizure stops, but Keith has cut his leg on the wheelchair, and he is dazed—as am I. Since I've never seen him or anyone have a seizure before, I think he's going to die.

The doctor follows Debbie to us, and he examines Keith while Debbie talks to the 911 operator.

I position myself between the stroller and my husband and dial Tiffini. "Please, can you come to the house to help with the kids?" I say in a quivering voice. "Keith's not doing well, the paramedics are on their way, and I think we'll be going to the hospital."

"I'm leaving now," Tiffini responds.

When the ambulance arrives, I stand halfway between my husband and my kids, giving the paramedics his health history and then turning the other direction to tell Debbie about Billy's food allergies, special milk, and how to get in the house. I climb into the ambulance while Debbie and another neighbor push the kids home to wait for Tiffini.

At the hospital, they give my husband seizure medication and then monitor him to see if it will be effective. When they admit him for the night, a neighbor swings by to pick me up. The plan is to go home, check on the kids, and then return to be sure my husband is settled in his hospital room. As I try to make sense of what's happening, I remember a conversation with a neurologist several months ago. He said some people who have had strokes often have seizures later. I had hoped my husband would be spared this side effect. Apparently not.

At home, Tiffini is playing with the kids, who are all smiles, so I head back to the hospital. When I walk into my husband's room, he tells me he has been throwing up. My heart sinks. Because of his issues with swallowing, he has a high chance of aspiration pneumonia if he vomits. It's something we'd hoped to avoid.

A few days later, he is released from the hospital. He sleeps more during the day, and it takes more energy than it should for him to get out of bed—all of which I attribute to new seizure medications and the stress of having been in the hospital.

By Friday morning, he is lethargic and has a fever. I contact his pulmonologist, who orders X-rays, and I drive Keith to the hospital. The X-rays indicate the aspiration pneumonia we'd feared. They start him on antibiotics. For the next few weeks, he is unable to attend any of his therapies. Simply using the bathroom tires him out. He had been doing so well. Keith was stronger physically, his voice was less raspy, and he had less difficulty finding the words he wanted to say. We are very discouraged.

A few days later, while my husband sleeps, I take Billy and Riley out for a quick walk in the neighborhood. Afterward, they eat a snack while watching a favorite *Barney* episode. Since today is a preschool day, I am preparing Billy's gluten- and dairy-free snacks when the phone rings.

"Hey, it's Tiffini. Are you watching the news?"

"No, I'm watching *Barney*."

"Well, turn it on."

I dash to the bedroom and turn the TV on while muting it so my husband can continue sleeping. I watch as they show footage of an airplane hitting the World Trade Center.

For the rest of the day, even when I'm not watching, I replay that video in my head. When Keith wakes up, he is glued to the TV, and all day long I see the incredible sadness in his eyes.

That night I can't sleep. Every time I close my eyes, I see the towers falling.

CHAPTER 14

When It Rains, It Pours

NANCY

I have no idea what's coming when my husband's fists fly at me. I'm driving him to a luncheon at his work that's being given in his honor to celebrate his progress. He punches me in the right arm several times. I take a quick glance in the rearview mirror at Riley. She's in the backseat moving her legs to the rhythm of the "Wheels on the Bus" song.

I grab Keith's arm. "Stop it, Keith. What are you doing? Stop!" I say as firmly as I can without risking upsetting Riley.

The punches continue to fly, even as I pull off the highway and stop the car.

I jump out, then march around to his side, my whole body shaking. I open his door. "Get out. Get out now. You cannot hit me when I'm driving. You can't hit me when I'm *not* driving!"

"What?" Keith looks at his hands. Then he looks back up at me in a way that I can tell he has no idea he hit my arm.

I don't know what's going on with him, but I can see he's shaken up. "I will get behind the wheel again only if you promise not to hit me. You can't hit me, Keith. Promise me."

"I promise."

I slide behind the wheel and continue our drive. We sit in silence as "Pop Goes the Weasel" plays in the background.

I'm still shaking as I pull into the loading zone and watch Keith walk into the building as if nothing had happened. Fifteen minutes later, I'm almost home when my cell phone rings. I pull over. It's Keith.

"I feel like I might be having a seizure," he says.

I hit the pedal and turn the car around. "Where are you in the building?"

"The lobby."

"You need to let the security guard know. Sit down so you won't fall."

I'm calm while I give him instructions, but my heart races as I speed back to his building. Although he has had several seizures, for the past few months his seizure medications have been effective.

When I pull into the loading zone, the security guard helps my husband to our car. He lies down, putting his seat back, and closes his eyes.

Later that evening, after the kids are settled for the night, I try to decipher what happened. I think the idea of the luncheon with his colleagues might have just been too stressful for him. It has been over five months since he set foot in his office, and I'm sure it felt overwhelming, given his limitations.

"Keith, maybe this afternoon was just too much for you." I rub his shoulder.

"Probably, but I wanted to go."

Inside, I'm still upset, but since I can chalk up Keith's behavior today to stress, I also assume that if I can keep his stress levels down, it may not happen again. I'm concerned about leaving on vacation the next day. I thought that would be good for us, but now I wonder how I'll manage his stress.

The next day, just before leaving town, we meet with our Realtor and drop the asking price on our house. It's apparent from the feedback that most buyers love the house and the view, but they're not happy that the main floor has only two bedrooms. Most potential buyers want all the bedrooms on the same level.

With all our responsibilities taken care of for now, we're excited as we pull onto the highway and head for San Diego. We're looking forward to spending time with both sides of the family.

The drive is long, but it's a fun new adventure. After a couple of nights in hotels, we check into our vacation condo. Although there still isn't a lot we can do as a family, I am enjoying a break from the work of showing the house.

Our third morning of vacation, just as I'm getting out of the shower, my husband appears in the doorway with blood running down his forehead. He has a strange look on his face and just stands there staring at me.

Grabbing a towel, I go to him. "You had a seizure."

He shakes his head no, but I know that kind of wild-eyed look he has. I settle him on the couch while I head to the bedroom.

The lamp is on the floor, along with the comforter, sheets, and pillows. There is blood on the corner of the nightstand. As I step into a pair of jeans and then slide a T-shirt over my head, I pace back to the living room, where I hear the words I'm dreading.

"I think I'm going to have a seizure."

Since he has never had two in a row, and since he has a gash on his forehead, I reach for the phone while holding on to him to keep him from falling off the couch.

After calling 911, I phone my parents.

"Hi, Mom, Keith is about to have a seizure, his second in a row. I need help. Can you and Dad come right away?"

"We're on our way."

The one thing I hadn't considered when planning this trip was the lack of help we'd have on an almost daily basis.

I place my hands on my husband's chest and pray as calmly as I can. "God, help us," I say over and over.

After a couple of minutes, we are pretty sure the oncoming seizure has subsided.

Billy and Riley are in the same room, but thankfully, they're occupied with watching one of their shows. Neither seems to have noticed their dad's strange behavior.

As I hold on to my husband, I hear vomiting behind me. Apparently, Riley had too many strawberries for breakfast, and now they're all over the carpet. After making sure Keith can sit on his own, I wash her face, throw a towel over the strawberries on the carpet, and return to Keith's side.

The paramedics and my parents arrive about the same time, and I follow the ambulance in my car to the emergency room.

Four hours later, the medical professionals increase his Dilantin to provide extra seizure control. When we get back to the condo, he sleeps the rest of the day and night.

The next morning, reality sinks in. Keith has to be seizure-free for six months to be able to drive, something he desperately wants to do so he can regain some independence. So this seizure episode is a major setback.

Unfortunately, he isn't just disappointed—he is also angry.

In the living room, he shoves me. "Now I won't be able to drive. I cannot go back to that house and be stuck in the neighborhood!"

He puts his hands on my shoulders and shoves me again with all his might.

I stumble backward. "Stop, Keith. Stop! Keep your hands off me!"

"Don't touch her again!" shouts my mom, who'd come again that day to help me.

But his hands land on my shoulders again, and he shoves me repeatedly.

"Keith, no. Stop!" I yell.

In an instant, I can almost see a switch going off in his brain. He tips his head as he looks from me to his hands. He realizes what he's done, and he plunks onto the sofa, head down, elbows on his knees. I decide to call Karl, one of Keith's lifelong friends who lives nearby, and he comes to get him. Keith spends the next couple of days with Karl while I try to figure out our next move.

After going over my options, I call Keith. "I think it would be best if you take the train to your brother's house and stay there for a bit. Take a break from me and the kids and our house. I'll fly home with the kids and do my best to get the house sold."

I intend to drop the price on the house further still, even if that means we lose some of our equity.

I spend the next two days searching for a rental home in San Diego. We need one near restaurants, stores, and a movie theater so Keith will be able to walk from our house. Before flying home, I sign a lease on a condo right across the street from a center with a bookstore, a movie theater, and restaurants. Even better, there is a physical therapist a half a block away. My husband will have places he can go on his own until he is able to drive.

Less than three weeks later, we are in negotiations with a buyer for our house. I call my husband and ask him to come home so we can pack everything for the move. We plan to have everything situated with the house and be on our way by the end of the month.

Then the rain comes. The news refers to the deluge as "the hundred-year flood." People all over the city are being evacuated.

Our split-level home is situated on a hillside, so we feel secure from the flood. But the rainwater soon becomes too much for the drain under our home. On the third day of rain, a neighbor friend and I look downstairs and see water rushing in under the stairway.

"I'll get some buckets!" I run upstairs to the utility room and grab two buckets.

She and I stand at the bottom of the stairs, trying to bail water out the side door, but it just keeps coming. My friend calls some other neighbors, and a group of them help us carry all the furniture up to the main level. By the time it stops raining, both downstairs rooms are damaged.

The restoration company is out early the next morning with gigantic fans. I feel certain we can get this repaired quickly and follow through with the sale. I contact our landlord in San Diego, and she graciously agrees to hold the condo for us.

Two days later, while things are drying out downstairs, I smell an electrical burn upstairs. I unplug appliances and try to figure out where the smell is coming from. I'm baffled, but I need to take my husband to a physical therapy appointment.

When I open the door leading to the garage, the smell overwhelms me. I call an electrician, and within thirty minutes he climbs down from the attic and says, "I don't want to alarm you, but you need to dial nine-one-one and get the fire department."

After I call 911, I take Billy and Riley to a neighbor's house and then return to see a fireman knocking holes in the dining room wall with an ax.

The insulation inside the wall is black. After the firemen leave, the electrician explains how he can isolate the breakers involved so we can safely stay at the house. I listen carefully to his explanation, but I cannot imagine staying here. I will not be able to sleep knowing that getting the four of us out of the house would fall entirely on me.

I call the Realtor and pull the house off the market, and we check into a hotel. I collapse into the bed while Billy and Riley watch *Blue's Clues* on their little DVD player.

The next day, while our babysitter watches the kids in the hotel room, I return to the house to gather more clothes and toys. In Billy's room, I notice that the cover to the electrical outlet near his bed is charred and melted. I call the electrician. After he inspects it, he turns off the breaker to the room.

Two days later, I return to the house and find a melted power strip in the kitchen. I call the fire department. They inspect and decide to shut off the electricity completely and red tag the house.

Of course. Keith's seizures. A flood. A fire. Why not. My perfect plan has dissolved.

CHAPTER 15

The Drive to Drive

NANCY

As Billy gathers up all his toys to take with him just for a trip to the grocery store, my heart breaks. He doesn't understand why we left our home, and he's not adjusting at all to living in a furnished apartment. I think he assumes he will never see his toys again, so we have to bring everything with us even for short trips.

We've tried to make progress with the insurance company for almost a month, but it becomes clear we need to move on. The insurance company is still looking into the cause of the electrical fire and refuses to allow us to start any repairs until they have determined the cause.

I just don't have the fight in me to deal with this on top of the medical malpractice lawsuit I filed a couple of months ago. The attorneys are hiring expert witnesses, and they have asked a lot of questions.

To make matters worse, the cost of the furnished apartment is double our mortgage payment. We've been getting by on savings, long-term disability insurance for Keith, and social security, but we can't pay out this much. After a month in the temporary apartment, we decide to turn the house over to the bank and lose our equity. We need a fresh start.

A group of friends helps us pack. There is no electricity in the house, so neighbors run extension cords with fans to help us keep cool while we throw stuff into boxes and load them into the U-Haul. We left one car in San Diego while we were on vacation, so the plan is for one of my husband's friends to drive the U-Haul to our new home. Our friend Joey will bring our second car later.

One of the first things we do after getting settled in our new home is look for a church. We've visited Hilary's church a couple of times and liked it. I want to know more about God, and what better place than church for that?

I find a church willing to let Billy be in the toddler room with Riley since he cannot go with his age group. Perfect! This church is similar to Hilary's church, and after leaving Sunday service, I feel refreshed. The pastor encourages us to bring a Bible to church, so I buy one.

The condo is also perfect for us. My husband can walk everywhere he needs to go. Once he makes the six-month mark seizure-free, he can take driving lessons. I'm secretly hoping the walking will go so well that he will forget about driving.

Unfortunately, that does not happen.

"Nancy," he asks one day, at almost exactly the six-month mark, "since I haven't had a seizure in so long, I'd like to drive again. Can we make that happen?"

"Sure, Keith. Let's go look at the car and figure out what we need to do." It would be so great if he could drive, but still, I'm apprehensive.

We have an accelerator pedal installed on the left side of the brake, which will allow him to use his left foot for driving since he has more control with that leg. He starts taking lessons with an instructor who specializes in drivers with a brain injury.

When Keith completes the lessons, he is cleared to drive. My heart pounds. On the one hand, I'm very glad he will be able to safely drive, since he really wants to. On the other hand, I see his daily challenges that lead me to believe this won't be quite as easy as we would like. For example, almost every day he calls me into the room to help him find something that is literally right in front of him. It's as if he looks everywhere except right in front of his face.

Sure enough, on his second day of driving, I receive a phone call from him.

"I'm in the parking lot at the grocery store," he says. "I really thought I had the gear in reverse. I did."

My heart sinks.

"But I hit another car and a fence."

I can then hear him talking with the other driver. I yell into the phone to get his attention. "Keith, Keith! Do not say too much. Exchange info with the other driver and then drive straight home." I wonder if I need to drive out there.

When he arrives home, I suggest he needs more lessons.

"No. It was just one time. I don't need more lessons. I'll be fine next time."

When I insist, he packs a bag and walks out the door.

"Exactly where are you headed?" I call after him, raising my eyebrows.

He pauses. "I don't know." He sets his duffel bag down and scratches his head.

"Just please don't go to Mexico."

It's a place he frequently talks about visiting. But if he has a seizure or another complication while in Mexico, I wouldn't be able to go get him.

He picks up his bag and starts walking. I'm angry, but I don't chase after him.

For two days, I hear nothing. Though I'm still angry, I also enjoy not walking on eggshells over the whole driving issue.

Two days later, I get a collect call from Cancun. Of course.

When he returns the following week, it's just easiest to go on like he'd never left. He takes more driving lessons, and again he is cleared to drive.

After a few months of driving success, I feel more at ease with his abilities. Our lease is up on the condo, and we are still in depositions for the medical malpractice lawsuit. Since we are unsure of when we will have the funds to buy a house, we decide to rent one.

I am excited for Billy and Riley to have a backyard to play in. Billy is attending a kindergarten class that specializes in teaching children with autism, and in the afternoons, he has a tutor who comes to the house to work with him. Two afternoons a week, Riley attends a preschool program. With my husband able to drive, living in a neighborhood does not place limitations on him.

And then one Thursday, while I'm standing in line at the grocery store, my phone rings. I don't recognize the number on the caller ID but answer anyway.

"Is this Nancy?" an unfamiliar voice asks.

"Yes, this is Nancy."

"This is Officer O'Neal from the San Diego Police Department. Your husband has been in a car accident. He's okay but is too shaken up to talk."

"Where is he?"

"At the corner of Mesa and Ninth. Can you come now?"

I leave the cart full of groceries and dash to my car. Along the way, I call the preschool and tell them I'll be late picking up Riley.

When I arrive in our neighborhood, I see that the front of Keith's car is destroyed, and the big truck he hit has a sizable dent on the passenger-side door. It's obvious that Keith tried to make a left turn but didn't see the truck directly in front of him.

My stomach plummets as I listen to my husband chatter about the accident.

"I never even saw that truck! How could I have missed it?" It's clear he is a danger to himself and anyone on the road.

Since we are now down to one car, he won't be able to drive even if he wants to. That gives me some time to think of a plan before breaking the news to him that he won't be driving anymore.

Fortunately, we have a diversion when we are called to give our depositions for the medical malpractice lawsuit. My husband's parents come to town to watch the kids while we fly out to meet with our attorney.

When we arrive, our attorney gives us an update on the depositions that have already taken place. Two nurses from the hospital have testified regarding the surgeon's previous "bad outcomes." They also testified about increasing the staff in the ICU for the days this surgeon performs surgery and about how they'd voiced their concerns on multiple occasions to the hospital administration.

Once again, I am shocked this has been allowed to happen.

The next day, I give my deposition while my husband waits in another room. I testify about Keith's limitations, his inability to return to work, and his struggles with daily tasks. I tell the lawyers that even though it has been over two years since his stroke, he still requires twelve hours of sleep at night; he often cannot locate an item sitting right in front of him; and though he reads simple books to our children, he has to guess at the words. I testify about how he doesn't have the ability to remember and follow through on plans. Nearly every day I realize he is more limited than I'd thought the day before.

"For example," I say, "in the morning, he ties a knot in his drawstring shorts. But at night, he asks me to untie it." I make a motion with my hand, as if tugging on a drawstring. "'Why don't you untie it, Keith?' I ask.

"'I can't remember how,' he says. Every time."

I note that if he carries anything in his right hand and fails to keep his full attention on that hand, he drops the item. He has no control over the volume of his voice, and he speaks so loudly, everyone turns to stare at him. He has no filter between what he thinks and what he says, and often he blurts out inappropriate comments.

When I am done, I feel bereft. Focusing on all his limitations at one time has taken its toll. During lunch with our attorney, I regroup by giving myself an internal pep talk.

Shortly after lunch, we enter the conference room for my husband's deposition.

The opening statement is given, and then my husband is asked to state his full name for the record.

"My name is Keith . . . Keith . . ." He clearly can't recall his middle name. He is stuck.

"My name is Keith . . ." he repeats, clearly hoping his middle name will come to mind. It doesn't. He shakes his head and tries again. Then he looks down at the conference table, and using his index finger on his left hand, he traces the beginning letter of his middle name over and over.

The attorney giving the deposition jumps in. "Are you trying to remember your middle name?"

"Yes. I know it starts with an E." Keith traces the letter again on the table.

"Take your time. No hurry."

"It's Nancy." He shakes his head, and says, "No, that's not it."

"Well, we can just use your first and last name. Why don't you state it for the record."

After a few more simple questions, the attorney wraps up the testimony, and we are free to go.

We return home the next day to see our two happy, sweet kids. I am so glad to be home and to have the pressure of the depositions behind us.

That stress may be behind us, but another resurfaces. Keith brings up driving again.

No-o! A bad idea.

In an effort to solve this dilemma, I decide we must move again. We'll move close to his parents, to the city he grew up in. I am hopeful that once we're there, he can reconnect with childhood friends. In doing so, possibly he will have a social life fulfilling enough to take his mind off driving.

Possibly.

CHAPTER 16

The Final Straw

NANCY

It seemed like a good idea. It really did. But it has turned out to be a huge mistake. It is too difficult for my husband to be back in his childhood hometown and not be the person he always envisioned he would be. Worse yet, he *had* been that person, but since his stroke, he no longer is.

I wish I had thought to pray before making this decision. I'm not sure if it would have helped, but maybe, just maybe, God would have told us not to make this move. I do think He answered my prayer when I prayed during Keith's seizures. I guess I'm just not sure if God will really answer my prayers all the time or just some of the time.

This move is not the answer we hoped it would be. His higher stress levels cause his seizures to return. The increase in his seizure medication causes him to be more tired. Being more tired causes him to become depressed. His depression brings on anger, which translates into stomping around, pounding his fists on the table, and yelling.

"In case you haven't noticed, I had a stroke. Enough was taken from me. You can't take my freedom too."

I'm back to walking on eggshells, trying not to upset him. I shield him from the kids and the kids from him. Unfortunately, shoving me when he is angry becomes a common occurrence.

He stays up late and gets up late, which becomes a good thing because that only gives me a small percentage of the day to manage the kids and him at the same time. We seek counseling. Each time the counselor attempts to set some boundaries on Keith's behavior, he quits counseling.

Although Keith is having trouble adjusting, the rest of us aren't. Billy's school is a good fit, Riley attends a preschool affiliated with her previous preschool, and I make friends with some moms from the preschool. We also find a wonderful church less than two blocks from our house.

Whenever I can, I spend time with Victoria, a friend who works at our church. She is the voice of reason and helps me understand the magnitude of the problems. She helps me to see clearly that I should not put up with the physical abuse.

I'm really torn. I would normally never endure someone pushing me, but he is brain injured and loses control.

In April, his former employer notifies us that it's time for an evaluation by a neuropsychologist. For him to continue receiving long-term disability pay, they need to assess his current level of functioning. Two days in a row, I drive him to an office for hours of testing. He is exhausted but feels like he did really well.

The report of the evaluation arrives in May. The good news is the long-term disability pay will continue. The bad news is the report details all his deficits: low memory, low problem-solving skills, low executive functioning. I wish I had been the one to bring in the mail so he wouldn't have even seen this report. He makes me read it to him. Although I can skip over some of it, he looks right over my shoulder and points to areas for me to read. I feel terrible for him, and I try to explain that the report is solely focused on his difficulties, not his strengths. But nothing I say or do seems to help.

Two days later, he has a seizure. I find him in the hallway and help him to bed. He sleeps on and off for almost twenty-four hours. When he finally gets up out of bed, it's evening. He is still out of it but wants to read a bedtime story to Riley. After an hour of his talking and "reading" with her, she is very tired.

I poke my head in the door. "It's her bedtime. She has preschool tomorrow."

"Just one more book," he says.

After they read through that book, Riley tells him she is tired and wants to go to sleep. He sits there with her until I peek in again. "It's past time for her to go to bed. Why don't you tuck her in?" I say.

When I head back to our bedroom, I can hear him in the hall behind me. As soon as we are in our room, he shoves me down on the bed.

"Keith, what's up—"

He jumps on top of me, pinning me to the bed. I knew he was unhappy about me setting some boundaries with Riley, but I hadn't expected this crazed-with-anger reaction.

"What are you doing? Let me up!" I am stunned but also scared. He has never done anything like this before.

"Let me go!" I twist and writhe beneath him, but he puts his hands on my throat. "What's going on?" I fight to get my words out as his grip tightens. "Get off me!"

He finally sits up, though he says nothing. He simply stares at me with an edgy look in his eyes. I am not safe.

He stays on the bed, but I jump up, grab my phone, and run out, dialing.

"Nine-one-one what's your emergency?"

Through tears, I whisper as loudly as I can so the kids won't hear. "My husband pinned me down on the bed with his hands around my throat."

"Where is he now?"

"He is in the bedroom."

"Okay. I will stay on the line with you until an officer arrives. Are you hurt?"

"No, I'm okay. I just don't want to be around him." The words coming out of my mouth sound like something I would watch on TV, not something I'm saying in real life. "My husband has a brain injury—that is why he lost control. We have two young children, who are in bed. Please be sure the car does not have flashing lights or a siren." I unlock the front door and wait silently on the phone until the police arrive.

Two officers question us separately as I keep an eye on the hallway to be sure the kids stay in bed. Afterward, the officers compare notes, and then one asks, "Do you want to press charges, ma'am?"

"I don't want my husband arrested, but I want him to leave. With his brain injury, he can't drive." I pace. I can hardly believe this is happening. I love my husband, but this violence terrifies me. It goes further with every incidence.

They call a taxi for him. I hand him his wallet and medication, and he leaves. All I can do is stare through the open door as he climbs into the taxi.

How has it come to this? I recognize I am in danger. I am not sure what to do from here.

The next day when he calls, I suggest we take a break. He decides to take the train to go visit his brother. I'm relieved and know he'll be safe there.

I'm waiting on pins and needles for his next call, and three days later it comes.

"Nancy, I'm ready to come home. I need to come home. I won't push you again."

"We can't just go on like this," I say. "But I don't want to give up either. Come back to the area, and we'll meet with your counselor and see what he says. But you can't come to the house."

Later that day, he calls me asking if I can give his friend John his passport. Keith is at the airport, planning a trip to South America. He traveled a lot for his job as well as before we were married, so I'm not surprised to hear he's planning a trip south of the border.

I have no idea how to solve this problem, so I pray—a still-unfamiliar response for me. I've heard pastors pray in church, and I remember the hospital chaplain praying, but I've never really prayed much myself. I just start pouring out my heart to God, hoping that maybe He will help me.

"God," I begin, "my husband is angry about his life, but I cannot live like this. I have worked so hard to keep us together. Why is this happening? Why won't You fix this? God, please help us so we can stay together as a family. I just cannot imagine us not being together."

The next day, my friend Victoria gives me two phone numbers. One is for a pastor who does counseling. The other is for a divorce attorney. I schedule meetings with both. The pastor helps me understand with complete clarity that this is not a tolerable situation and that my kids might even be in danger if Keith's behavior escalates.

Although I'm reluctant to see a divorce attorney since I really do not want it to come to that, I still go through with the meeting. The divorce attorney asks me to bring a list of all the times my husband has been physical and to include dates. During our meeting, he looks at the pattern and tells me I am in danger. The incidents have been escalating in seriousness and are happening closer together. Both are bad signs. For the safety of myself and the kids, he suggests I do not allow my husband to return home.

Fortunately, I am able to track Keith's location in South America through ATM withdrawals. Although I see our money being depleted from our account, it also brings comfort. While he is still far away, I have time to figure out my next move. I am having a hard time figuring out if I should stay or move back to San Diego.

It helps that we recently arrived at an agreement with the attorneys over the malpractice suit. While nothing can reinstate the life we once had or make up for the suffering we've all endured, we're glad it's over.

I schedule a trip to San Diego over the July Fourth weekend, to see my parents and some friends. My good friend Gwen invites us to stay with her and says she'll help me look for a rental house. On the drive, I pray and pray and pray. I look in the rearview mirror at my kids' faces. They are so young, and I cannot believe I am considering leaving their dad. On the other hand, I know I must. *God, please help me. Please show me what to do. Make my decision clear to me.*

Gwen has already set an appointment for us to see a nearby townhome for rent. Her husband watches the kids while we check it out. The area is perfect, and the townhome is exactly what we need. In addition, we already know a family in the neighborhood with a daughter Riley's age.

By 3:00 p.m. I have signed the lease. God has shown me exactly what to do and where to go. The kids and I are moving to San Diego without Keith. I'm feeling both stunned and relieved.

CHAPTER 17

Finally, Peace

NANCY

When my phone rings unexpectedly, I tense up. So often an unexpected call has meant nothing good. When I see that it's Keith, my body stiffens even more.

My husband has returned from South America to find that we left a few weeks ago.

"Keith, what else could I do? Things were escalating between me and you, and I am worried about the kids." I pace in the hallway.

"I want my family with me!" Keith says, clearly angry.

"We will plan visits with the kids," I reassure him. "I promise you that. I'm not trying to keep you from the kids. I just want us all to be safe and healthy."

"I want to come down so we can talk about this in person."

I agree to meet him at the church so we can talk together with the pastor about all this. Once the pastor explains that for Keith to move back in with his family, he'll have to make changes, Keith rises and walks out.

He leaves town again.

At home, I sink onto the living room sofa and plop my stocking feet onto the coffee table. For the first time in a long time, I feel complete peace. My mind is still. My heartbeats are regular. My breathing is even.

Everyday life is so much easier. I did not realize how difficult it had been trying to keep the peace. The kids and I are much more relaxed.

Once Billy leaves for school each morning, Riley and I have the day to spend together. Some days we have fun at SeaWorld or the zoo, but we have just as much fun going to the grocery store. I did not ask for this freedom—I'd just kept going, going, going—but now I feel the weight of the world lifted off me.

One day while Riley and I are in the car, running errands, I bring up our new living arrangements. "Daddy is not going to live with us anymore. He really needs everything to be quiet, and you know how loud Mommy can be."

"Oh, yes, Mommy. You are loud sometimes."

"Daddy will still come to see you. We can go to the park or the pool together, so it will be fun."

"Okay, Mommy."

We drive in silence for a couple of minutes, and then she says, "Is he going to go live in the forest?"

I smile. "Probably not. He will just live in a house by himself. Grammy and Grandad will keep him company sometimes."

"Okay, Mommy."

Over the next few months, Keith comes for occasional visits, and I'm with him and the kids at all times. If things don't go Keith's way, he gets upset, and I run interference when needed.

Sometimes we meet at Disneyland or a park, and he is always better behaved at public locations.

An unbelievably peaceful year passes, though, of course, life with a child with autism rarely has many dull moments. I'm glad I have a good sense of humor, especially when the unexpected occurs. One of our fun outings is going to Carl's Jr. I order Riley's milkshake, then retrieve Billy's non-dairy milkshake, which I brought from home. I pour it into the empty milkshake cup the cashier is kind enough to give me.

Milkshakes in hand, we head outside to the play structure. There are tubes and tunnels, and at the end is a fun slide that they both *whoosh* down. Usually Riley goes first, with Billy right behind her. She jumps up quickly at the bottom to avoid having him slide right into her. This is a skill she developed early on, and she knows its importance. However, this particular day it does not go as planned. Riley exits the slide, but Billy is not behind her.

"Riley, where is Billy?" I try to peer into the structure.

She shrugs, then runs off to enter the play structure again. I wait, and soon here comes Riley again.

She then tells me, "Mommy, Billy is just sitting in the tunnel. I said to him, 'Come on, Billy, follow me,' but he stayed in the tunnel. You might have to go get him."

Go *get* him?

I bend down again to look into the tunnel, but I can't see him. After calling his name and trying to coax him down, Riley and I end up having to climb up into the structure and through the tunnel, saying "Excuse me" to the other children as they move out of the way of a forty-year-old woman crawling on her hands and knees.

When I finally emerge with my son in tow, I can't help but laugh.

A week before Halloween, we come home to find a note on our front door saying, "You have been booed," along with a basket of fun Halloween treats. The note has instructions on how to go about booing your neighbors. I decide this could be fun, so I make up a couple of baskets of Halloween items. The next afternoon, I get Billy in a stroller so the three of us can deliver the baskets to a couple of neighbors. The idea is to leave them quickly so no one knows who delivered it.

This part of the plan does not go smoothly at all.

Each time I try to leave one on the porch, Billy jumps out of the stroller, runs up to the door, and retrieves the basket. After a few attempts, we head for home, along with our two baskets.

Never a dull moment.

This reminds me of the first year I was brave enough to take Billy and Riley trick or treating. I did not realize, until it was too late, that even though I explained what we were doing, the concept was a bit beyond Billy's comprehension.

We approached the first house—Riley dressed as a bumblebee, Billy as a pirate, and me in my usual mom attire. Feeling pleased with myself for getting us this far, I boldly knocked.

The door swung open to a woman wearing a pleasant expression and a pair of cat ears.

Before any of us could say anything, Billy pushed past her, right into her living room. Making himself at home in the empty recliner, he began watching the TV.

After apologizing and scooting past the shocked homeowner, I coaxed Billy out of the house while thinking, *This is clearly an issue we will need to address before next Halloween.*

CHAPTER 18

Getting Help

NANCY

One Sunday morning, we enter the church and make our way through the crowd of people gathered in the lobby. After checking Riley into the first-grade room, Billy and I find a spot in the hallway to watch the service on the TV screen.

Although Billy settles on my lap for a few minutes, before I know it, he is up moving around. I follow after him while doing my best to hear the message. Finally I sit on the floor leaning against the wall and coax Billy into my lap by offering him some snacks. While we're sitting there, a pastor walks by. She stops, then turns around to talk to us.

Thinking she's about to tell us we can't sit in the hallway, I jump up, ready to explain our situation. But instead of giving us a reprimand, she is very kind and suggests we should meet to see if we can figure out a way for me to attend service without having to sit in the hall.

I give her a quick explanation of autism as she hands me her card. We make plans to meet for lunch during the week to see what we can figure out. I'm excited at the idea of attending the service, but I also know that the past accommodations of allowing Billy in the toddler room will no longer work. Billy is now eight years old and tall—far too tall to be in a room with toddlers. Other than the toddler room, there really isn't a place for him.

When Pastor Sarah and I meet for lunch, I explain the struggles we have with Billy and how we are not alone. There are many families like ours who are not able to attend church. This really sets her wheels in motion. She is determined to provide a way for families like ours to be included. We discuss the idea of creating a special space for children with autism and other disabilities that will allow the parents to attend church.

Within a few months' time, we open the space and advertise in the community. Within a few weeks, over twenty new families are attending church. With some wonderful volunteers, we are able to staff the room with almost a one-to-one ratio. Each week, I am so happy to see the looks of gratitude on the faces of parents who have been wanting to attend church for years but just haven't been able to.

Several weeks into the new program, I notice in the announcements that the church has a caregiver relief group. I circle it so I can remember to call on Tuesday and get more information.

Wouldn't it be great if we had some volunteers from church to help out and give me a break?

I am already so grateful for the friends I have, like Lisa. I met Lisa when we first moved back to San Diego with Keith. She has a son Billy's age, and we really have fun together.

I call about the relief group and make arrangements for them to come help us.

From this point forward, every Saturday two volunteers show up. I'm so happy when the weekend rolls around and I have caregivers coming to help with Billy and Riley. This means that instead of doing stuff with the kids, Lisa and I can actually go out to lunch together.

The relief group becomes an even bigger blessing to us when we meet Karlee. She is wonderful with both Billy and Riley. We quickly fall into a routine of having Friday night movie time with her. Billy, Riley, and I go to Blockbuster on Friday afternoons to select the movies. When Karlee arrives, we make popcorn and settle in.

We are also blessed to meet Kristie. Kristie brings her daughter to play with Riley. When her daughter and Riley become friends, Kristie starts bringing Riley to her home to swim and play.

Our community is expanding, and so are our blessings. Then another unexpected blessing comes along.

One weekend, a pastor I hadn't met before visits our special-needs ministry. He seems very interested in it. He introduces himself as Pastor George. As he and I discuss what a blessing this is to our families, to my surprise, he says he would like to know how he can help us. Is there anything these families are in need of?

My mind races as I consider the many needs we have. I explain all the extra planning that goes into even the ordinary events in life—like, for example, having repairs done in our homes. I explain that we must be sure the repair person understands the need to be quiet and not make any abrupt moves, to be careful if they leave to go to their truck; to please be sure to close the door all the way. Then, as the repairs are taking place, we are often faced with shocked looks as our child makes squealing noises. It can really wear us out.

When the pastor says he would love to help our families by completing small repair jobs, I am thrilled. He then suggests that I pave the way by accepting help myself.

I'm a little overwhelmed by the offer. It just feels too good to be true, but who am I to question it?

On Thursday morning, Pastor George and another man from the church show up to repair some of my kitchen cabinets with dangerously loose hinges. All I can think while they work away is *Thank You, God!*

This is exactly what families like ours need.

Over the next few months, Pastor George and a few volunteers help with needed repairs and odd jobs for several of the single moms. It isn't often that someone outside our special-needs circle shows such an interest in being with us, so I consider this to be a blessing. Pastor George asks me questions and seems genuinely invested in being as much of a blessing as he can.

As he works and asks questions, I share what I can about the difficulties we face, especially us single moms. He often responds by quoting a Bible verse or a passage that fits with our situation.

My response—since I know very little—is usually "Wow. Is that really in the Bible?"

Pastor George calls me often to check in. He wants to know how each of our families is doing. I find myself thinking, *This is how it should be—a community of people helping those who need it.* What a great church! I'm not surprised at all when one of our special kids ends up in the hospital and Pastor George shows up to visit, not just once, but several times. I am so grateful!

One morning after dropping Riley off at school, I call him to ask if one of the volunteers could take a look at my garage door, which is sporadically stopping midway up or down. Although so far, I have been able to hit the remote again and get it moving, I'm worried that it may stop working altogether. He says he will be right over to take a look, and within the hour, we are standing in my garage talking while he works.

By now, we know each other pretty well, so it seems perfectly normal when he asks how Billy's new school is working out and wants to know what part Riley has in the school play. What does catch me completely off guard is when right after our hug goodbye, he leans in and gives me a quick kiss.

Uh . . . *what?*

As I watch his car pull away, I stand there stunned. What just happened? This is a pastor, and not only a pastor, but a *married* pastor. What was that?

The next time he arrives to help, he brings a volunteer, and it's just business as usual. They complete the job, and as he's leaving, he gives me a quick hug and apologizes for the kiss. He tells me he is going through some rough times and slipped up, and he is very sorry.

I'm relieved. Our families need him, so I'm grateful to know we can continue as if it never happened.

The problem is, several weeks later, it happens again.

Having talked myself into feeling safe with him, I share a little too much of a struggle I'm having in a situation with a friend, and he gives me a hug. Feeling grateful for the comfort and hug, I stay there a little too long, and as I pull away, he pulls me back toward him straight into a kiss.

Stunned and confused, I just stand there while he gathers up his repair supplies to leave.

Later that day, as I replay the whole thing in my head, I realize that it's been a while since any of the other volunteers have been by to help me. It's always George. And although I thought that was a good thing, I now realize it's not a good thing at all. I wonder what I said or did that led him to believe I wanted more than help with household repairs.

I'm not sure what to do, but I do know I need to figure it out. I certainly hope none of the other single moms are facing this situation. I remember that initially the plan was to have two volunteers working together, so I take some comfort in that. Most likely I am the only one George is helping alone. I know I need to be sure I am not alone with George again.

The problem is, George is calling me a lot. Although the conversation usually begins with discussions about the needs of the families, including mine, it almost always ends up with us talking about George's life and problems. He has problems with the other pastors. Apparently, he is very misunderstood and mistreated, not only at church but also at home. I listen and try to help the best I can. Unlike George, I am not able to share any Bible verses. I do not know the Bible like he does. He reassures me that just listening to him is a big help. I feel good that I can help him. It feels like the least I can do since he is helping us so much.

The next time we meet, it's to discuss a project for another special-needs family. He wants my input as to how to best help. However, the conversation once again quickly turns to his problems. As we sit and try to sort through some of them, he pulls me in for a kiss. Now I know there is a big problem.

I stiffen, not knowing what to do.

He makes an exaggerated show of shifting back, holding me at arm's length. "Uh . . . Nancy . . ." His expression is a mix of unreadable emotions. "I think we have a problem here."

Relief washes through me. He recognizes that his behavior is causing an issue.

"I agree," I say, expecting him to admit that he's behaved badly and that he can't come to my house alone anymore.

He clears his throat. "I think you may need to step down from leading the special-needs ministry."

What?

I don't even know how to respond. I just know there are so many families depending on this ministry, and I cannot let anything happen to it. How could I have been so stupid? All I wanted to do was to bring help to families like mine. Now, that seems to all be at risk.

I don't know what to do. I need to explain to George that I never wanted anything more with him than some help, but I also need to figure out how to explain it in a way that doesn't hurt him.

The following day as I'm folding laundry, I ponder how to best separate myself from George. I'm not at all sure why he thought I wanted to be that involved with him, and the last thing I would ever want to do is add to his problems. But that seems to be what I have done. I replay some of conversations and interactions to try to understand how I led him to believe I wanted anything more than friendship.

While I put away the last of the folded clothes, I receive a call from Pastor Sarah. She informs me that Pastor George met with the other church pastors and shared about our inappropriate relationship. The pastors want to meet with me as soon as possible. I agree to a meeting that evening at my house after Billy and Riley are in bed. Mortified,

I hang up the phone. I think about the whole situation while waiting for Billy's bus.

What in the world is wrong with me? I am not someone who goes after married men, but somehow that is exactly what I seem to have done.

After Billy and Riley are both tucked in that night, I sit in my little living room with three pastors. They share what George told them and ask if it's correct. I hang my head and tell them that, yes, it's correct. We kissed, and it was more than one occasion. Pastor Sarah tells me that I cannot be part of running the special-needs ministry. I feel so ashamed. I cannot believe this is happening.

Later, as I try to go to sleep, I'm sick to my stomach. I think about the special-needs families and the team of volunteers. Who will run this ministry?

The following week, I receive a call from Pastor Sarah. She would like to have a meeting with one of the elders from the church. We set it up for the following day.

As we sit down with our coffee, the elder informs me that I will no longer be allowed to attend church services. Although George has resigned from his position, his children attend the church, and they want it to be a safe space for them. He then tells me that my children are welcome also, but I can no longer come into the building.

I nod as tears run down my face. I feel so ashamed about what I have done.

By the time I arrive home, I can barely think straight. I am completely devastated. Almost everything about my life revolves around this church. All my friends are there. I helped create the special-needs ministry to be able to go to church, and now I cannot even go into the building.

Why, God?

For the next few weeks, I go through the motions of life with the kids, but my head continues to spin. Why would God allow this pastor into my life? Why did He allow something that seemed so good to go so badly? What am I supposed to do now?

One afternoon a few weeks later, Pastor Sarah calls again and asks if she can stop by.

During our conversation, she asks me, "When did you receive Jesus as your personal Savior?"

Caught off guard, I respond by telling her, "I'm not sure. I guess when I started going to church again. I mean, I grew up Catholic, but I don't remember anything about Jesus being a personal Savior." She asks if I would be interested in doing a beginner's Bible study together. It sounds good to me, especially since I have no ability to attend church services anymore.

Over the next few weeks—as I begin to learn what it actually means to accept Jesus as my personal Savior, and some very simple truths from the Bible—I realize how much I didn't know and how much I've been missing out on.

Pastor Sarah asks if I would like to join one of the women's Bible study groups. Starting in the fall, there's going to be one at the church on Monday mornings, and if I would like to attend, she will get special permission for me to enter the building. I tell her that I would love that. At this point, I will take crumbs. I feel so stupid for derailing my whole life.

Once again, I replay everything with George in my head. What did I say or do that told him I wanted more than house repairs? I'm still not sure, but I do know I never want to be in a situation like that again. If studying the Bible can help me with that, I'm all in.

Pastor Sarah tells me that the Bible study starts the first week of October. Perfect! The kids will be settled back in school by then, and with special permission granted, I will be able to attend this women's Bible study.

I find myself wanting to know more now, so I pray and ask God to help me comprehend the Bible better. I have read through the book of John. I now understand that Jesus is the way, the truth, and the life (John 14:6), so I want to know more about Him. I also want to check out any teaching on wisdom so I can be wise enough to avoid situations like the one with George. I certainly never want to be kicked out of a church again.

Even in my Catholic faith, I never felt like I was at risk of being kicked out of the church. I know that if I am ever allowed to return to church, I want to be sure I know enough and can be good enough.

One night, after Billy and Riley are in bed, I set out to find all the reasons the Christian church would ask someone to leave. I figure if I know what those reasons are, I can avoid making any mistakes. Maybe I can even meet with the pastors and explain that I now understand. Maybe then I can return to church, to my friends, and one day be good enough to run the ministry again.

As I search my Bible and ask God to direct me to the information I need, I find Matthew 18:15–20, where Jesus gives the steps involved in church discipline. Perfect! I take a quick break to switch the clothes from the washer to the dryer, and then sit back down to study this section.

What I find is not what I expect at all! It turns out, there are multiple steps involved, and all for the purpose of restoring the sinner to a right walk with God. The first step is to address the sinner in a one-on-one setting. Then, if the person is unrepentant, the next step is bringing two or three others. If there is still no repentance, the matter is brought to the church.

If after the third opportunity, the person is still unrepentant, church discipline or removal from the church may be necessary. The overall goal of church discipline is the restoration of the individual to full fellowship with God and other believers.

Wait . . . *what?*

I look it up on gotquestions.org, just to be sure I am reading and understanding this correctly. My situation was not handled this way at all. I was never unrepentant. I never thought what I did was okay.

Why was the first meeting with three pastors? Why after that meeting was I kicked out of the church? I cannot understand this at all.

By the time I calm my brain enough to try to sleep, it's already eleven p.m. It's too late to call Pastor Sarah, but I really want to know why I was kicked out. Why wouldn't they follow what the Bible says?

The next morning after breakfast, I get Billy off to school. While Riley plays in her room, I call Pastor Sarah. I ask her about the way my situation was handled and why it wasn't done the way the Bible says it should be.

She pauses, then says she doesn't know.

I hang up, thinking that if this church didn't follow the Bible in my situation, are they not following it in other situations? This not only strengthens my desire to know more from the Bible but also leads me to believe that this church may not be the church I want to attend. I have a couple of months of summer before the women's Bible study begins, so I decide I'll learn as much as I can between now and then and enjoy my summertime with Billy and Riley.

We do have a great summer. Billy leaves for his short school days each morning by 7:40, and Riley and I use that time to either go to the beach or play at the park. When Billy arrives home, we have a quick lunch followed by a special adventure like an afternoon at the community pool or a trip to the wild animal park. Most evenings, except for Friday movie nights, are spent reading the Bible.

I am very much looking forward to this Bible study in the fall.

CHAPTER 19

Riley's Big Question

NANCY

It's mid-September. Riley is now in second grade, so she has plenty to talk about on the drive home from school. One day she climbs into the minivan, puts her seatbelt on, and instead of telling me about the games she played on the playground or what she learned in math, she asks me an unexpected question.

"Mommy, when do I get my stepdad?"

Caught off guard, I say, "What do you know about stepdads?"

"Well, Makayla in my class got her stepdad, so I want to know when I will get mine."

I take a deep breath. "Well, stepdads are kind of like babies—they come from God. So we just have to wait until God brings the right person to be your stepdad."

"Okay. Can I have a milkshake when we get home?"

"Yes, one *huge* milkshake coming up!" *Please don't ask me about stepdads again.*

I left Keith two and a half years ago, and our divorce was finalized a year after that. I'm not considering dating again. I met Keith when I was twenty-two and was with him until I was almost forty.

Once we are home, she has her milkshake followed by dinner, homework, a bath, and bedtime stories. During all this, I start thinking that perhaps I cannot just rely on God to bring a stepdad to our front door. I might have to do a little dating to make this happen. Since it has been over fifteen years since I have been in the dating world, the thought is overwhelming.

A few days later, I call my friend Tracey. She is also a single mom of a son with autism. She tells me all about how much fun she is having with online dating, and she offers to help me create my dating profile. Maybe it would be fun, but I cannot imagine it. The next time we talk, she brings dating up again.

"Let's post some pictures and write your profile. It'll be fun!"

"Well . . . I could use some fun, but I don't have any pictures that are just of me." *Oh well, I guess I won't be online dating after all.*

"No problem; I'll pick you up in the morning. We can go to the beach and take pictures."

"Okay, great." *Oh geez, I guess I'm really doing this.*

The next morning, I throw on my jeans and sweater, and we head to the beach. Later that day, my pictures are uploaded, and I sit down at my computer to work on my profile. The first thing I do is look through some of the profiles on the site. It becomes clear that my answers are going to be different from most. I'm not traveling, I'm not having weekend getaways, and I'm not attending concerts or going to clubs. I'm at home with my kids. That's about it.

What a weird idea, to put all this information online.

There are categories and questions to answer for my online profile, and I know I'm going to have to get creative with my answers. I mean, what do you list for favorite travel destinations when you don't travel? In the end, my humor takes over, and I just answer the questions honestly:

FAVORITE TRAVEL DESTINATIONS: *Costco and Target.*
FAVORITE HOT SPOTS: *In front of the oven, while taking out the chicken nuggets and french fries.*

I include a few paragraphs about what I'm looking for, and I include the things I like about being single:

I can have popcorn and wine for dinner if I want to.
But it might be nice to share the popcorn and wine after
having dinner together.

A few days later, I have Riley take some additional pictures of me on our front patio.

"Make sure you only see me from the waist up," I say, since I'm wearing sweatpants and slippers with my blouse and cute little jacket.

I work on the profile a bit more. My goal is to make it clear that my kids are my top priority while at the same time making it clear that I do want the right person to join us. Then I hit the button to publish it.

What have I gotten myself into? I feel so unprepared for this.

Much to my surprise, within a couple of hours, email responses file in. The typical one reads:

I really like your profile, and I think I'd like to meet you.

Tracey is right—it is fun to read the profiles and respond to the emails. I exchange phone numbers with some of the men.

Most nights, after Billy and Riley are asleep, I have phone chats and learn about the men who have emailed. I have to figure out if they truly want a simple life like the one the kids and I have, or if they're thinking I'm willing to have two lives—one with them and one with my kids. I start a little journal with the conversations so I can keep the details straight.

A couple of weeks later, I drive to a restaurant for a dinner date. About halfway there, I realize I'm more than a little nervous about the idea of dating again. When I arrive, we shake hands and talk, but I start to feel kind of shaky and begin to hyperventilate. We sit down on a bench outside the restaurant so I can catch my breath.

My date asks me, "Is it me? Is it me?"

"No, it's not you," I reassure him. "I just . . . I just need to get used to this whole idea of dating again. Sorry this didn't work out tonight, but I need to head home."

In the car, I find a music station to distract me. After a couple of minutes, a song comes on. I've never heard it before, but there's something about it that stirs my heart. Tears are actually blurring my vision to the point where I have to pull over, which gives me the opportunity to read the song title and artist on the reader board on the dash. "I Will Be Here," by Steven Curtis Chapman.

If I ever really start dating, I think, *this is the kind of man I'm going to look for.*

After a few dates, I kind of get used to the process. I like hearing other people's stories and learning about their lives even when they are not a good fit—and so far, none of them are.

"What is your strangest online dating experience?" I ask Donovan while we sip coffee.

"It was basically a job interview to see if I would make a good date for her brother's wedding."

I ask that question almost every date, and wow, I hear some really good stories. In fact, I could write a book just from those stories.

Right before Thanksgiving, I receive a simple email from a guy named Jeff:

I like your profile. If you want to, call me.

He gives his phone number. I read through his profile, which has little information and only two pictures.

I like his pics, so I figure, why not respond. I send him an email:

I would love to talk with you. Here is my number. Call when you have a chance.

The following afternoon, my phone rings.

It's Jeff.

We talk nonstop for about thirty minutes until I hear Billy's bus coming up the street and have to end the call.

My stomach flutters each time he calls over the next four days. I find out his wife passed away a few years ago. He has two children, a boy and a girl. They are close in age to Billy and Riley. We talk about important stuff, like how heartbreaking it is being a single parent. But we chat about the fun stuff too, like where we grew up and what our childhoods were like.

Then we decide it's time to meet in person. We set up a lunch date for the following Tuesday.

CHAPTER 20

Dating Goes Awry

JEFF

What I miss more and more every day is conversation. Sure, I have the guys I play poker with and the guys I sit with at Charger games, but I really miss my conversations with Charmaine. Dating has little appeal—I've already done lots of it. I had a wife and I have kids—I'm not supposed to go through this whole process again. And I don't want to get married again—it seems too hard. Plus, when I'm off work, I want to spend time with Colin and Jessica.

But going out for dinner and conversation sounds nice.

I hear an advertisement on the radio for a matchmaking service, so I sign up for it. When the company matches me with someone, they set up a blind date. The only thing I know going in is the woman's first name. Since all the initial legwork is done for me, this seems like a good plan. I can meet someone for a meal and conversation and then head home to my kids.

The only problem is, after a few months I realize the "matches" are not good matches for me. When I'd wait at the restaurant and a woman would walk through the door, I was either thinking, *Yes, let it be her*, only to watch her greet someone else, or *No, no, no*, followed by "Are you Jeff?"

During a dining experience with one match, the whole lunch revolved around her dog—which sat in her purse at the table with us.

"What kind of dog is your favorite?" she asked.

"Umm, uhh, umm . . . I don't really have a favorite."

"Well, my favorite is, of course, my sweet little Maltese." She removes the dog from her purse and kisses it all while speaking to it with baby talk. Followed by dog stories, all told by her.

The shallow conversations leave me feeling let down. I wonder if I should arrange my own matching.

I search the internet for a different dating service and find Match. com. I can add information about myself and what I am looking for in a match. The cost is substantially less than the dating service, so I have nothing to lose.

I set up my profile, add a picture of myself, and look through the profiles of the women. If one looks especially pretty and at least mildly interesting, I respond. Writing has never been a strength of mine, so I end up sending a few emails:

I like your profile. If you would like to talk, please call me.

I add my phone number and hit Send.

After a few not-so-great dates, I am second-guessing the entire online dating scene. The women seem to want to move quickly. One is nice and easy to talk with, so after a few dinners out, I invite Ellen to my house for a casual home-cooked dinner. I dropped my kids off at my in-laws earlier that afternoon.

She arrives a few minutes before 7:00 p.m., her hair and makeup casual but pretty.

"Ellen, come on in!"

I open the door for her, and she enters, looking around like it's a house she's in the market for, not a companion.

Crossing to the sofa, she tucks a lock of hair behind her ear. "It'll be nice to relax in here with you after a stressful day at work."

Saying nothing, I set a pan on the stove for the noodles.

"Very nice." Surveying the room, she starts to chew her lower lip. "Er, except for the tile. Not really my style. Would you be willing to change the flooring?"

What? Umm, how do I even respond to that?

I feed her and end the night as quickly as possible.

On one of my rare second dates, another woman asks, "When do you want to get married?"

Rather than saying, "Possibly in fifteen years," I just say, "I'm not really sure."

Not the answer she was looking for.

With that kind of track record, I log out of Match.com and take some time off from dating.

But as Thanksgiving and Christmas approach, the toughest time of year for me, I rethink that decision. Although I'm used to spending the holidays with just the kids by now, it would also be nice to go out with someone.

I log in to the site and scan the profiles again. *Oh, what do we have here?* A funny profile snags my eye. Her name is Nancy, and I like her down-to-earth profile and pictures. Her references to Costco and Target amuse me, as does the oven for her favorite hot spot. She clearly has a sense of humor and doesn't get out much—like me. I read through her profile a couple of times and think, *Maybe I'll email her.*

Then Jessica comes into the room to say good night, so I quickly log out.

Later in the evening, after both kids are tucked in bed, I log back in to send that email. I cannot find her profile. Did she delete it? Where is it? It takes me a few minutes to find it again, and when I do, I send off my standard email:

> *I like your profile. My name is Jeff. Call me if you would like to talk.*

I add my number and hit Send.

The next day, she emails me her phone number and says she would love to talk. Smiling, I grab my phone and head out to the backyard to call her.

By the end of the week, we have had several great phone conversations, and we decide it's time to meet. I suggest we meet for lunch on Tuesday at Panera Bread. I'm looking forward to meeting her so much that I find myself thinking about our conversations throughout the weekend.

Tuesday morning, I send her a quick text:

I cannot wait to meet you today. See you at 11:30.

She responds:

Can't wait.

Around 11:00, I finish up a couple reports for work and make sure I am on my way to Panera Bread by 11:10. I am usually on time, and I do not want today to be an exception. I find a parking spot near the middle of the lot and sit listening to the radio until 11:25. I watch women walk into the restaurant. None of them look like her, so I'm either about to be disappointed or she just isn't here yet.

I lock my car and go inside to wait. While I'm sitting at a table facing the door, I look up each time it opens to see if it's her. My phone starts to ring. It's her . . . I hope she isn't canceling.

"Hello?" I hope I don't sound too anxious.

"Hi, it's me, Nancy. Are you here?"

"Yes, I'm here." I scan the room, looking for a woman on her phone. "Where are you?"

"I'm outside—can you come out? What color shirt are you wearing?"

"I'm wearing a red shirt." Standing, I shift my focus to the part of the parking lot I can see through the front window. "You can't miss me."

I hold the door for a couple of women walking in, and then I step outside and face the parking lot.

I see her walking toward me. She has a big smile, and my first thought is *She is really cute.* She is also confident—I can tell by the way she moves toward me that she knows who she is.

She gives me a quick hug and whispers, "Thank you for looking like your pictures."

We talk for an hour and a half. It's effortless. We share dating stories and laugh so hard that neither of us touches our food. By this point, I am wishing we had met for a drink instead of lunch. I casually mention that we should have met for drinks.

She looks at her watch. "We have time. Let's go."

Is she joking? As she stands up and grabs her purse, it's clear she isn't joking. So she's attractive, has a good sense of humor, is confident, and is spontaneous too?

We take her car a couple of blocks to a restaurant with a bar. After Nancy orders a glass of wine, I order a soda. I have to return to work at some point this afternoon. We have a great time talking, and when we leave an hour later, both of us really wish we had more time. After a hug goodbye, I tell her I will call her tonight. And I mean it.

CHAPTER 21

Dating

NANCY

Even though we have spoken on the phone for hours, I am nervous about meeting in person. I throw on my jeans and what has become known as my "dating sweater"—a loose-fitting black sweater I wear on my first dates. I do not dress up too much or overdo my hair or makeup. The men either like me or not.

Unfortunately, I've had a few dates where the person did not look at all like the photos that were posted. When that happened, I couldn't help but wonder what else they were not being honest about. So as I pull into the parking lot, I call Jeff.

"Hi, it's me, Nancy." I hope I sound enthusiastic but not too anxious. "Are you here?"

"Yes, I'm here. Where are you?"

"I'm outside—can you come out?" A little frazzled, I add, "What color shirt are you wearing?"

"I'm wearing a red shirt—you can't miss me."

A moment later, a man wearing a red shirt steps outside, and he looks exactly like his pictures. *Whew!*

I get out of my car and head toward the front door and the man in red. He gives me a quick hug, and we walk inside to order. After finding a secluded table on the outside patio, we sit and talk. He is exactly the same in person as he was on the phone. We spend two hours just talking and laughing. He jokes about neither of us touching our food and says we should have met for drinks.

I look at my watch, calculating how long I have till Billy's bus arrives at home. "We have time." I pick up my purse. "Let's go."

We spontaneously find a nearby restaurant with a bar, and I enjoy my glass of wine as we continue our conversation. Wow, I really like this guy. He has a great sense of humor, and he's super cute. Afterward, we return to Panera Bread, and I ask where he is parked so I can drop him off.

"I'm over there." He motions in a vague way.

Now I am curious. "Do you not have a car? Am I going to see you ride off on a bicycle? Or will I see you at the bus stop? Is your mom coming to get you?"

Looking kind of embarrassed, he points more directly to the far end of the parking lot, where a shiny red Corvette sits all by itself.

Not sure if he's being serious, I give his arm a playful backhand.

Raising his eyebrows, he reaches into his pocket and pulls out a set of keys. "It's my 'dating car.'" He holds up what is indeed a Corvette key ring.

We both laugh, and I realize even more how much I like him. What a great date.

Later that week, he asks for my address so he can pick me up on Friday night. When I tell him where I live, we are both surprised. He lived on my street years ago, before I moved to the neighborhood. I ask him if he ever went to one of the block parties.

"No, they didn't have block parties when I lived there."

"Oh, that's why they call them the 'Yay, Jeff moved out of the neighborhood' block parties."

He laughs. "Very funny."

Before our first "official" date—dinner, rather than lunch, coffee, or drinks—on Friday, he sells his Corvette and buys a new car.

He shows up right on time, he opens the car door for me, and we easily pick up our conversation again. *This guy just might be the real deal*, I think.

He takes me to his favorite restaurant, opens the door, has a reservation for the perfect table, and does all he can to make me feel special. We spend the next three hours enjoying great food and sharing life stories. Before the end of the evening, he tells me that the next time we come here, he wants me to try the salmon.

My heart races. *So there'll be a next time.*

After we talk for the whole drive home, he walks me to my front door and kisses me. It's the perfect kiss, the kind that says I really like you and respect you.

What a great date.

Since it requires a babysitter for me to go on a date, and mine isn't always available, we spend the next couple of weeks talking on the phone each night.

The next evening that I have a babysitter, I am overdue for dinner out with Riley. We like to do this every couple of months, and since Billy is not a big fan of loud restaurants, he rarely joins us. When Jeff asks me out, I mention that I'm taking Riley out for dinner this Friday night, but the following Friday I will be available for a date.

"That is a great idea to take Riley out. I think I will take Jessica out for dinner on Friday too," Jeff says.

Riley and I have only a couple of places we dine out at. She likes the Elephant Bar, since they have good desserts, and she likes Friday's, since they have ice cream with gummy worms. As we're being seated at our table at Friday's, I see Jeff sitting a few tables away with a little girl who must be his daughter. Neither of us mentioned the restaurant we were going to.

When he comes over to say hello, we invite them to join us. Riley and Jessica have a great time coloring pictures together and playing with Riley's toy camera.

While we say goodbye in the parking lot, I mention that maybe Jessica can come over sometime to play with Riley. Both girls are excited at the idea.

The following Friday, while Jeff and I go out to dinner, Jessica spends the evening at my house with Billy, Riley, and our sitter. When Jeff picks her up after our date, she says she had so much fun and wants to play with Riley again.

A few days later, Jeff asks me if I can get our sitter every Friday night. We decide it might be a good idea to have all the kids at my house with our sitter. So we tell Colin about my new computer with a fast internet connection, and he is all in. He will bring his war video games with him to my house.

Jeff and I have some things in common that make it easy to connect. We both have been asked by previous dates, "Which weekends are your kids gone with their other parent?" "None" is not the desired answer. We also do not have the freedom to get away for a weekend, ever. Since we have both been through a tragic past with our spouses, we understand it well, along with knowing what it's like to be a full-time single parent.

Best of all, we both have the same wacky sense of humor. I find it hilarious that when dates ask him how long ago his wife passed away, he often says, "Her funeral is next week, so I'm looking for a date to go with me."

After a few months of Friday night dates (which we decide to call meetings so our kids won't know we are dating—we don't want them disappointed if it doesn't work out), we discover that one of our favorite things to do is people watch. I have always been curious about people's stories, so when we see a couple at a nearby table, we try to determine whether they are on a first date or not. If we can overhear the conversation, we try to determine how well it is going. Or we cringe at what we hear and the body language that follows.

One Friday night, we are sitting at our table when Jeff mentions that he thinks he has spotted a first date.

I turn around to see the couple, then rotate quickly back to Jeff. "Oh my gosh, I went on a date with that guy! He asked me out for lunch. I had a salad and water, and then he didn't pay the check. It was really weird. It turned into kind of a standoff. I couldn't believe he had asked me out and then wasn't going to pay for my seven-dollar salad. So I just kept talking and talking while the check sat there. After the server came back twice, I finally put my money in the folder. It was so weird. I'm not opposed to paying for my meal—it was just the way he went about it."

When it is clear that the couple's date is wrapping up, I ask Jeff to watch and see if he pays the bill. Sure enough, he pays the bill.

When his date heads to the restroom and he is passing by our table on his way out, I just can't help myself.

"Doug, hi!"

I have caught him off guard. He stops, and after I introduce him to Jeff, he says, "I have been meaning to call you."

"Oh, that's okay. I just saw you and thought I would say hello."

The world of online dating is so strange, but it makes for some entertaining times for Jeff and me.

Jeff then tells me one of his dating stories. He had a date arranged through the matchmaking service. As he sat in the restaurant waiting, a woman approached him and asked if his name was Mike.

"No," he said smiling, "but I wish it was."

Although his date ended up being a no-show, the following day he was scheduled to meet someone new. When he arrived at the restaurant, he saw the same woman from the day before enter. This time, she was his date.

Ahh, the small world of dating.

I can't help but be very grateful that it didn't work out with her, or any of the women. I consider it their loss.

After we finish our dinner and the server clears everything, I look at Jeff and ask, "Are you ready?"

He looks at me and then casually reaches up and slides the folder with the check in it toward me. We both laugh as he puts his credit card in the folder.

I love that he gets me.

CHAPTER 22

Breaking Up Is Hard to Do

NANCY

Sitting in Bible study, I glance over at the woman next to me and notice that her Bible looks very well read. She even has highlighted areas and notes off to the side.

I know more than I ever have after these past few months of reading and studying, but I also recognize how much more there is to know.

I do wonder how much I really *need* to know. I do know I want to go to heaven when I die, and in my Catholic faith I learned that the way to possibly get there is to lead a good life, go to church every Sunday and all the holy days of obligation, obtain all the sacraments, go to confession with a priest, keep the Ten Commandments, and say the rosary daily. But even if I were to be successful in all of that, I would still most likely go to purgatory and hope that others would pray me into heaven. I now understand that none of those things will get me to heaven. I now understand from the Bible that admitting my need and accepting Jesus as my personal Savior is the only way to heaven.

Growing up, when I compared my life to the Ten Commandments, it became pretty clear I just couldn't do it. Even as a child, I knew I was failing at keeping them, and in my religion, that meant my chances of making it to heaven were very slim.

When I was a child, every Sunday as I stood on the patio after church service, I felt queasy—almost too queasy to eat the donut my dad had bought for me. I knew I was not good enough, and it became clearer each week that I would probably never be good enough. Why did God give us all these standards to live up to when, as hard as I tried, I just couldn't do it?

I remember my friend Anne talking about the Bible as if it is her go-to book for answers in life. I am beginning to understand just how important this book is, but I also realize the more I learn, how little I know. I realize how different it is from the religion I grew up in.

All these questions swirl in my head as I join this Monday-morning study. I'm welcomed into the group, and the women are so kind and caring that I feel right at home. Even though I'm clearly a beginner who knows almost nothing of what is being taught and discussed, I do feel that I'm exactly where God wants me.

The more I learn in my Bible study, the more eager I am to know even more. Instead of using the hour in between dropping Riley off at school and the start of my Bible study to run errands, I find myself wanting to sit in the coffee shop and go over my homework and notes from the previous week.

This particular week, I have just settled in at my table when I get a text from Jeff. He's wondering if I have time for coffee, so I invite him to join me.

Ten minutes later, I smile as he approaches my table with his coffee and tell him a little bit about where we are in the book of Daniel.

After a few minutes of discussing my study questions, he casually asks if this weekend I am free to go out not only on Friday night but also on Saturday. Since we're having such a great time together, I tell him it sounds good to me.

Then I start to wonder if we may be getting more serious than just casual dating. I really need to find out if he's looking at the future of our relationship the same way I am.

"So . . ." Moving my Bible aside, I lean an elbow on the table. "You really think you can handle seeing me two nights in a row?" I add a little laugh. "I mean, up until now, you've had some recovery time in between our dates." I'm kidding, and he knows it, but it's kind of a lead-in for me to see if he wants to be serious.

"I think I can handle it," he says, chuckling.

Still not sure, I take a sip of coffee and dive in. "There's something I'm wondering about."

He looks up, clearly not expecting my question to be serious. "What's that?"

"Well, you know, part of why I'm dating is because Riley really wants a dad. So, I'm wondering if you can see yourself getting married again?" When his face drops, I quickly add, "I'm not saying, necessarily to me." A chuckle comes out sounding tense. "I know it's way too soon for that kind of decision. I'm just wondering about your long-term plans."

Jeff takes a drink of coffee, probably to buy himself a moment before responding. "I do think I will get married again . . . one day. But probably not until my kids are grown."

"Oh, okay." I do some quick math. "That's . . . what? About thirteen years from now?" I throw in a playful roll of my eyes.

Looking serious, he slowly nods. "This gives me a lot to think about."

"What do you need to think about?" I'm trying to sound lighthearted so I don't come across as needy or demanding, but I can't help adding, "Thirteen years is a long time to just date someone. Can you even imagine the look on Riley's face if I tell her she'll get her stepdad when she's twenty?"

Although we both smile at that, I also know what this means. I need to start dating again while Jeff and I become "just friends."

We finish our coffee and hug goodbye, and I head to my Bible study, both excited to be there and feeling a little disappointed about the Jeff situation.

When Jeff calls later that afternoon, I break the news to him. I let him know that I really do not want to wait thirteen years to get remarried. If I don't find the right person, that's fine, but I'm not dating just to date.

Jeff, on the other hand, makes it clear that all he wants for now is someone to share dinner and conversation with. He's not ready to get serious with anyone.

I have to accept that, of course. But it makes me a little sad.

But then, something else hits me.

"You know," I say, "Riley and Jessica are pretty good friends. It would be unfair to take that away from them."

"True . . ."

When he doesn't offer a suggestion, I continue. "Can we agree that no matter what happens with us, we'll let them remain friends?"

"Good idea. I'm glad you thought of that."

Over the next few weeks, I struggle to get over my disappointment. I respond to a few dating emails, have some phone conversations, and go on a handful of dates.

In the meantime, Jeff and I meet for lunch a couple of times a week, and the girls continue with their playdates.

One day when he comes over to pick up Jessica, we catch up on life, once again over coffee.

"How's the dating going?" I ask as I refill his cup.

"Not very well." He frowns, and his fingertips drum on the table. "I'm not getting any responses."

I've adjusted to our just-friends status, so I offer to help him rewrite his profile and take some new photos of him.

Weeks later, he's still not getting any responses, so we sit down together to look through the profiles of the women on the site. I am shocked by what some of these women are wearing—or not wearing. And I can't believe how many profiles talk about candlelight dinners and long walks on the beach. And traveling . . . don't even get me started about that.

It's like they all want to live in a romance novel. Don't any of these people have to *work?*

Jeff and I end up spending a couple of evenings at my house looking through the profiles. I'm certain that if I can find just one normal person, he can go out and have a decent time. I really want him to be able to move on. What if I meet someone, and it turns into a serious relationship . . . and Jeff's not even dating? It might get difficult, and I don't want him to be sad if I get involved with someone else.

One evening, Jeff brings dinner, and while the kids are playing in another room, we sit down to read through profiles again. Finally, all my hard work pays off.

"I found her! She is normal sounding." I motion him toward the screen. "You should email her."

"Eh . . . maybe." He tips his head as he views her photo.

He isn't as enthusiastic as I am, but we create an email, and I hit Send.

Apparently, our email sparks an interest; she responds the next day. Since Jeff does well with conversation but not so great with emails, I help him draft his reply. Before we know it, she has agreed to meet him.

But I can see by the look on his face that we have a problem. "Uh . . ." He looks at me with scrunched-up eyes. "I've changed my mind."

"It's okay, Jeff." I put a reassuring hand on his shoulder. "She sounds nice. She's fully clothed! She likes the simple things in life. Why not meet her for coffee?"

"I just really don't want to." He rubs the back of his neck.

"Well, great . . . that is just great."

I'm not super surprised since Jeff wasn't excited about her to begin with, but I feel bad for her. She did everything right, and now she'll wonder what she did wrong.

"We don't want to insult the poor woman." I tap a finger to my chin. "I know—let's get *her* to change her mind." I reread her profile. "Let's see . . . She loves the outdoors, hiking, and camping. Hmm . . ."

I backhand his arm. "I know. We should email her about your lack of love for outdoor activities."

Which is true. He's not a fan of camping and hiking. Jeff latches on to the escape plan. Together, we write:

> *Maybe we can meet somewhere indoors. I am not big on the outdoors.*

Almost immediately, she emails back:

> *Sure, no problem. I do hope you like spending some time outdoors. I'm really a big fan of everything about nature. Just let me know where you want to meet. Looking forward to meeting you.*

Jeff and I respond:

> *Good news. I am working on enjoying the outdoors. I made it all the way out to my mailbox today. I hope I can one day stay outside a little longer.*

She makes us wait for her reply, but the computer finally *dings*:

> *I have been thinking more about whether or not we are a good match. I do so many outdoor activities that I think we wouldn't be a good fit. I hope you will continue to work on enjoying the outdoors—you really don't know what you are missing.*

Whew! Mission accomplished. Clearly, I am probably not the best matchmaker for Jeff.

But if she was so great, and he didn't go for her, who will capture his attention?

CHAPTER 23

Slowing Down on Speed Dating

NANCY

"I'd love to go out with you on the fourteenth, but not as a Valentine's Day date," I say to Craig, a guy I've gone out with a few times. "Just a get-to-know-each-other date."

He's nice enough, but we are not anywhere near being valentines.

We go to a movie and then head to dinner just across from the theater. He grabs my hand as we cross the lot, pulling me right next to him. This is sweet but a bit abrupt.

At dinner, he gives me not one but two Valentine's Day cards. It seems odd since I made a big deal emphasizing this is not a Valentine's Day date.

The next weekend, my friend Tracey and I sign up for a speed-dating event. In theory, it sounds fun. Just a few minutes with each person, then you switch tables. After meeting all the men, you write yes or no by their names. If two people both say yes, the event planners connect you.

The first guy sits down, and after we introduce ourselves, he asks, "Do you believe in ghosts?"

What?

I waste precious moments staring at him before I respond. "I'm guessing this is important to you? Why?" I don't really want to know, but it seems like the right question.

The remainder of our time together, he goes on and on about ghosts. *Ding* goes the bell, and I move on to the next guy.

Unfortunately, the rest aren't much better. Logan is recently divorced and seems angry.

Angelo is a lawyer, but instead of asking me anything, he just tells me all about his current case.

Jordan cries and tells me how sweet I look. His tears creep me out.

All in all, it's just plain weird.

A few days later, I go on a third date with John, whom I'd met online. Our first date was a quick but relaxing lunch, and he seemed like a nice guy. For our second date, we met for brunch by the beach. This third date is different. He seems serious and is trying too hard. It isn't relaxing or fun.

After dinner we talk in the parking lot, and then he says, "I love you."

Wait. What?

I'm so caught off guard that I give him a little punch to the arm and say, "Well, I love you too" in a lighthearted, goofy voice.

The following week, after Jeff and I meet for coffee, we head to a bookstore to browse the new releases—we're both into bookstores and love to read. Jeff loves thrillers. I love memoirs. We catch up, and he asks me how the dating is going.

"Well." I assume a mock-boastful expression. "There was my date with 'I-love-you John.'"

Letting out a little chuckle, he frowns. "Who?"

"John." I roll my eyes. "He said he loves me on our third date." Jeff shakes his head in disbelief.

"And Craig is out. He doesn't listen. Our Valentine's Day was a total flop." I describe our walk from the theater to dinner and tell him about the cards.

"Brother." Now it's Jeff's turn to roll his eyes. "Why is it so hard to find someone who's just . . . normal?"

As we leave the bookstore and head across the parking lot, Jeff grabs my hand and abruptly pulls me right next to him, reenacting my date. We both crack up.

Man, I really like this guy!

Jeff, that is. Not Craig.

I feel like taking a break from dating. It's getting tiresome. I'm also noticing that many of the men who checked the Christian box on their profile are not truly Christians. It reminds me of the process of selecting a church. Although the website sounds good, it isn't until I actually see whether or not the teaching is from the Bible and accurate that I know if it's the real thing. When I ask about their faith, or how long they have been a Christian, quite often the guy has no answer or an answer that shows me they just checked a box that they thought sounded good

When Tracey calls a couple of weeks later and invites me to a speed-dating event run by a different company, I tell her I need to think about it.

A few days later, I have coffee with Jeff at the shop near Riley's school.

"I'm thinking about trying another speed-dating event." I raise my eyebrows as a thought occurs. "You want to join Tracey and me?"

"If you go, I will go with you," he says, to my surprise. Okay—this could be fun! Anything Jeff and I do together is fun.

The next Saturday evening, Tracey, Jeff, and I are sitting in the bar at the restaurant where the speed-dating event is being held. Just before it starts, Jeff and I look at each other.

"I don't want to—"

"—do this—"

"—do you?"

Tracey gives us a good-natured roll of her eyes and heads into the event, leaving Jeff and me to have a drink and people watch.

Even though my dating life is rather tumultuous—when it's not nonexistent—I continue to be amazed by what I am learning from the Bible. Every time I glean something new, I am stunned at how different it is from the religion I grew up with. Several times a week, I call one of my friends and say, "Can this be true?"

Lily has been studying the Bible for years, and her answer is always the same. "Yes, it is true."

For example, I grew up believing I needed to do a whole lotta work perfectly to have the slightest chance at heaven. And you really wouldn't know if you had done it all well enough until after death.

That is some religion—one that offers no peace.

When I study the book of Luke, I am struck by the exchange between Jesus and a criminal being crucified next to Him.

The man says to Jesus, "Lord, remember me when You come into Your kingdom."

Jesus responds, "Assuredly, I say to you, today you will be with Me in Paradise."

Again, I call Lily and ask if this is true. Can someone go directly from here to heaven? Especially if they are a criminal?

You see, in my religion, those of us who are less than perfect will end up in a place called purgatory. In fact, during the church services I attended while growing up, we prayed for the "poor souls in purgatory." So wouldn't this criminal hanging next to Jesus at a minimum have to go to purgatory for a while?

Lily and I go a few rounds in our discussion, but she insists there is no mention of purgatory in the Bible.

"The Bible," she explains, "teaches that spending eternity in heaven with God is a gift, not earned. All we have to do is receive it."

What? I don't think I have ever rejected a gift. Why would I?

Especially when it's the greatest gift ever. Seriously, it is a gift God gave us, through Jesus.

But as I'm learning, I can't help but wonder—are there conditions to this gift? It does sound too good to be true.

As I learn more, I discover there *are* some conditions. First of all, I must admit my need by admitting that I am a sinner. At first, I feel a little angry about this. I'm a pretty good person, and I have tried my best my entire life to be kind, do the right thing, help people when I can, and make sacrifices for other people, so admitting I'm a sinner? What exactly does that mean? I've never committed any crimes, I've never intentionally done anything terrible, so why in the world would I need to admit to being a sinner?

What I discover is that we are all sinners. The Bible says that every single one of us falls short of the glory of God, so that makes us sinners.

I then think about what my sins are.

Have I lied? Yep.

Ever stolen anything? Yep, I stole a little Avon perfume from a friend's house when I was eight.

I begin to realize that it really doesn't matter to God if I stole perfume or a car, it's the same, stealing, which means I'm a sinner—someone who's not living up to God's expectations. I also know that my interaction with Pastor George certainly falls short of God's standards.

Then I find out that even our thoughts make us sinners. Okay, well, in that case, I can admit I'm a sinner. I do know I have never measured up to God's standard. In fact, that is the reason I completely gave up on my religion from childhood. I could never be good enough.

Now, there it is, in black and white. The Bible says we are all sinners, but God has made a way to be with Him by having His Son, Jesus, pay the penalty for our sin—my sin—and for that I'm grateful. It turns out that all those years I was trying to keep the commandments and be good enough, that was something I could never do. God, knowing this about me, sent His Son, Jesus, into the world to live a perfect life and then die for me, paying the price for my sin. This allows me to know for certain I will be in heaven. My sin is no longer counted against me.

When I realize this and accept Jesus as my Savior (the one who died in my place), I feel a freedom I have never felt before.

These verses really make sense now:

For God so loved the world that he gave his one and only Son, that whoever believes in him shall not perish but have eternal life. (John 3:16 ESV)

For by grace you have been saved through faith. And this is not your own doing; it is the gift of God, not by works, so that no one can boast. (Ephesians 2:8–9 ESV)

I sit curled up on the sofa, my Bible open on my lap and my highlighter in hand. Really? It's as simple as accepting a gift rather than working for eternal life? I now understand that there's no way I can do anything good enough to get into heaven except believe in the Lord Jesus Christ.

Until now I had always ranked people based on how "good" they were when it came to religious activities and church attendance. And I truly believed some people were more deserving than others of being in heaven with God.

That is not the case. It is based on a gift, not our works. I like this!

I'm excited about all the spiritual discoveries I'm making, and I enjoy my Bible study group on Mondays more and more. Since I grew up in a religion that taught me to believe in things that are not in the Bible—like praying to Mary or praying to saints or the idea that a place called purgatory exists—I begin to wonder about other religions. Do they also use some of the Bible and then add to it? In the Catholic religion, when we say the rosary, most of the prayers are to Mary. Sure, Mary had an important role in this world since she was chosen by God to give birth to Jesus, but Mary is human, just like me.

I then recall a conversation I had with a friend right after Keith's stroke. She said, "I do not believe Jesus is the only way to heaven."

Since I really knew nothing at the time, my response was simply a nod. I guess at the time it did seem like a loving God would give us many options. The truth is He is a loving God who gave us everything we need to know in the Bible for wise living here and for eternity. But He also gave us free will, and with free will, we can reject His ways. Since I now know that the Bible is the truth and that Jesus is the way, I don't want anything else.

As I'm leaving Bible study one day, a bumper sticker catches my eye:

Smile, God loves you.

I really wonder about that. I see some happy women in my Bible study, so I'm sure they are doing something to allow themselves to believe that God loves them.

For me, it's different.

As a child, I never felt that God loved me. I felt like He was disappointed in me. I can accept now, based on the truth of the Bible, that God loves me enough to give me a way to spend eternity with Him, but in my everyday life, I don't often feel loved. I know my kids love me, and I love them completely, but life is hard. I'm a single mom of two kids—one with autism—with hardly any money. And I don't see God making it that much easier. If He loves me, wouldn't my life be easier?

I hop into my car to head home. Maybe at the house I'll see what the Bible has to say about God loving me.

After dinner and putting the kids to bed, I finally settle in with my Bible. What I discover is that in addition to loving me enough to die for me and give me the ability to spend eternity with God the Father, Jesus also promises to send a helper, the Holy Spirit, to those who choose Him. I learn that the Holy Spirit resides in me now to help me in this life. The Holy Spirit is the one who gives me the peace I have during the super trying times, like the day of Keith's surgery.

I dig deeper, and I also learn that nowhere does the Bible say that life will be easy. In fact, as I study the lives of the people in the Bible, I discover that there are many who had difficult lives.

When Jesus was speaking with His disciples, He said, "These things I have spoken to you, that in Me you may have peace. In the world you will have tribulation; but be of good cheer; I have overcome the world" (John 16:33 ESV).

As I continue to flip through the Bible, just before drifting off to sleep, I come across Romans 8:28: "And we know that in all things God works for the good of those who love him, who have been called according to his purpose."

Wow! The Bible really does address everything and provides all the answers we need. I am still carrying the shame of not only what happened with Pastor George but also the shame of not being able to attend church. When the women in my Bible study begin to talk about the weekend message, I feel such guilt and shame about not being able to be there and to know what they know. I know I don't deserve to be there, but I am hoping this verse will give me some insight as to whether it is fixable. I mean, someday I would like to attend church service again, and knowing that the Bible may provide answers gives me hope.

Knowing that God will work this together for my good allows me to drift off to sleep. Knowing all that brings peace to my heart. But life is still hard.

CHAPTER 24

The Heart Will Find a Way

JEFF

It's Friday afternoon, so I leave work a little early with a plan to pick up pizza on the way home. I'm hoping Nancy will want to come over with her kids, and since I haven't talked to her in a couple of days, I call her on the way to my car.

"Hello?"

How is it that just the sound of that one word makes my day brighter?

"Hey. It's been a few days since I've heard from you." Hoping I don't sound needy or demanding, I quickly add, "How is everything?"

"Everything's good."

There's a clattering sound in the background, and I can tell she's in the middle of doing something.

"Just busy with stuff." She goes on, though she's obviously a little distracted. "Riley's playdates. Everything Billy needs. And of course, laundry and cooking." There's a pause, then the sound of what must be either the washer, the dryer, or the dishwasher. "How are you?"

"Great." I unlock my car, not sure why I'm suddenly a little nervous. "I'm just leaving work, and I was wondering if you and the kids might want to come over for pizza later? I should be home around four, if that works for you."

"Oh . . ."

There's a long pause, and the sound of the washer, dryer, or dishwasher grows distant. I lean on the top of my car, picturing her walking from room to room picking up toys, and it's oddly comforting.

"I'm so sorry," she finally says. "We can't make it tonight. It's a great idea though. I hope you have fun."

"No problem." Opening my door, I squash an undeniable urge to ask her what her plans are for tonight. "See you Sunday, then?"

We've made a regular habit of them coming over on Sundays for swimming and a barbecue. But it strikes me at this moment that we've never talked about it as a standing date. It's just kind of turned into that lately.

"Yep," she says. "We'll be there."

We exchange a few more niceties, but I hang up feeling awkward. What are her big plans for tonight? I'm pretty sure she's going on a date. Otherwise, she would have told me.

As I get into my car and start the engine, I give myself a mental reprimand. I really don't like the idea of her going out with someone else, but I also know that it makes sense. After all, I told her I don't want to get married until my kids are grown. For all intents and purposes, our just-friends status looks pretty much the same as what I would look for in a dating relationship at this point. But Nancy wants something more. It's completely reasonable for her to keep dating other people.

I shouldn't feel . . . what? Not *jealous*, certainly. Shaking my head, I back out of my parking space and start for the exit. I'm not jealous.

I'm *not*.

However, the more I think about it, I have to admit that I do not want to live life without her, and that very well could happen if she meets someone. It's just so hard.

"*Why* is it hard?" I mutter to myself, tapping the steering wheel as I wait for a light to change.

I know I resolved not to remarry yet, but for the life of me, I'm not sure why.

The light turns green, and my muttering continues.

"The kids would have to adjust."

That sounds rational, but even I know that's not a problem. Colin and Jessica already adore Nancy, and the ease they have with Riley and Billy makes them seem like siblings already.

"One family would have to move." True. But is that really a dealbreaker?

"I don't know if I'm up to parenting a child with special needs." But even as I voice that concern, I know that's not enough to write off Nancy and her family. It's taken some getting used to, but Billy's a great kid. Being a single parent is tough, and wouldn't it be easier for two parents to manage four kids than for each of us to handle two on our own?

I spend the rest of the drive wrestling with my sense of uneasiness with the prospect of getting married again. So much about it sounds great. Why can't I put my finger on the problem?

After grabbing a pizza, I arrive at the house and pull into the driveway next to my parents' Buick. It's a familiar sight since my parents and Charmaine's alternate days being at my house to take care of Colin and Jessica after school. They've been such a great help, and I love that they can feel connected to the kids.

I take the pizza from the passenger seat and head inside. My mom fills me in on what she and the kids did today and what she and Dad are planning for the weekend.

A few minutes later, I'm in the kitchen grabbing plates out of the cupboard and thinking how great it would be to have Nancy here setting the table and telling some funny story about her day.

"Dad! Hey, Dad!"

Colin interrupts my thoughts. I give him my full attention as I set the plates on the table and the kids take their seats.

"Dad, today in PE, we were playing basketball, and I threw the ball. I really thought it was going to go into the basket, but instead, it bounced off some girl's head."

Jessica starts laughing, but I hold up a hand to shush her. "What? Is she okay?"

"She's fine." He shrugs. "Just surprised. You shoulda seen her face."

He follows that up with what I assume is an exaggerated impression of the girl getting beaned with the ball, which makes Jessica laugh even harder. Before we know it, all three of us are cracking up.

A half hour later, after clearing the plates and throwing out the pizza box, I head into the living room, where the kids are looking through our DVD collection trying to agree on a movie for us all to watch. Once again, I begin thinking about how much I want Nancy in my life—permanently in my life, and as more than a friend.

As the kids hash out the benefits of *Toy Story* versus *Ice Age*, I try not to think about Nancy being out on the town with some other guy. Okay, okay. Maybe I *am* a little bit jealous.

I decide to shift my thinking. What if instead of listing the reasons against remarrying, I think of the reasons *for* it?

I settle back into the sofa. Of course, it would be great to have another adult around. A good friend to do life with. Plus, she's a stay-at-home mom, so that would relieve both sets of grandparents from their caregiver duties.

No sooner does that thought enter my head than a pain hits my gut—a pain that I know has nothing to do with the half a pizza I just consumed.

As Colin puts the movie into the player—looks like *Toy Story* won out—and Jessica settles in next to me, realization sinks in. That's the reason I've been resisting remarriage. Both my parents and Charmaine's parents love being needed and being a part of the kids' day-to-day lives. I cannot imagine taking that away from them.

But at the same time, I do not want to lose Nancy.

It's about time my hardheaded self admits that I've fallen in love with her.

CHAPTER 25

Living with Autism

NANCY

Bible study isn't the only meeting I go to, but it is my most enjoyable. One of my least favorites is our IEP (individualized education plan) meeting. Ever since Billy started school at age four with a diagnosis of autism, at least once a year I meet with the team of people who work with him. We look at progress and goals for the coming year.

It's painful to hear about all his challenges and lack of progress in a two-hour session. Even though I live with it daily, it's still hard to hear, especially when his life is compacted into such a short amount of time. And even though I see all the special things about Billy, none of those traits translate to school success. Although the team does its best to include positive things about his school day, most of the meeting is spent discussing the gut-wrenching concerns. The boy I see as the most gentle, loving person with a fantastic sense of humor is viewed differently in the school world. The people sent to assess him often have never met him, and a test with a stranger never goes well with Billy. The results are almost always negative and very clinical.

In school, the fact that he struggles with sensory overload makes most of his day difficult for him. In these meetings it's apparent that at most, he takes one step forward, often followed by four or five steps back. If he made progress in, say, identifying coins, the next time he is given this task, he just simply cannot do it. Instead of it being a fun game for him, he could just as easily toss the coins onto the floor out of frustration. Or if it's a rough day, he will just quickly match the word *dime* with the picture of a quarter. Often he just wants to be done with the task, so matching incorrectly is not of any concern to him.

He has extreme anxiety, and none of the possible solutions we try seem to help. One teacher has suggested he rub a rabbit's foot when he feels anxious. But Billy doesn't feel the anxiety coming on; it quickly overcomes him and puts him in fight-or-flight mode.

As I talk to Jeff on the phone the night before this year's upcoming dreaded meeting, I share how hard it can be to sleep, knowing what's coming the following day.

"Could I go with you?" Jeff casually asks. "If you want me to, that is."

"Wow, really? You would do that?" Support would be so great. "I don't know that I could really help since I've never been to an IEP, but I would love to go with you."

"I would love that too!" My voice shakes. "Just to have someone by my side would be amazing."

The next morning, he picks me up—while some kids attend their own IEP meetings, this isn't a good idea with Billy, so he takes the bus to school—and we drive to the meeting together. Oh my gosh, I already feel a huge weight lifted off me. These meetings can be so emotionally draining that even driving home afterward is just too much. Now I have someone to drive and to sit with me!

After the meeting, all he can say is "I had no idea. I had no idea that parents have to go through that. That was tough."

"Yep. Welcome to my world, and oh my gosh, thank you!" I know I'm gushing, but I'm just so grateful. "Thank you for being willing to come with me and for wanting to be part of my world. You just took one of my most trying days and made it a little bit easier." Actually, a lot easier.

In the bigger world, where I am frequently reminded of everything I'm missing out on, it's overwhelming and sometimes lonely since people with kids who don't have autism often cannot understand us. Their kids are driving them crazy with their questions, or soccer practice three times a week, art classes, and homework make their lives so busy. All I can think is *I wish I had those problems*. Everything I do has to be planned to the smallest detail, with backup plans.

What breaks my heart as much as Billy's struggles in this world is the complete lack of acceptance we face. I know that not everyone knows Billy has a disability. He looks very typical, and it's easy for people to just assume he's misbehaving. Unlike a physical disability, autism cannot always be seen. It often shows up as random and unpredictable coping behaviors that Billy uses to get through each moment.

When he's getting his hair cut, for example, he sits in my lap and watches a show on a VHS tape. This salon caters to children, so they have a good variety to choose from. This is great while we are there. However, he wants to take the videos with him when we leave! Once I have him in the car, I gather the tapes—which makes him angry. I usually wind up tossing the VHS tapes through the door to the stylist.

And quite often, the more extreme the situation, the more extreme the coping behaviors Billy will use. And the more likely it is that people will judge.

A good example happened back when Billy was five. Keith, the kids, and I were on an airplane returning from Florida, where we'd seen a neurologist. The airport wait had been long, with many more preboarders than normal. By the time we made it to our seats, Billy was stressed. Unfortunately, he did not have the words to tell me anything.

Before the flight had even taken off, I was already over halfway through my large duffel bag of toys. I knew he was doing his best to calm himself, so when he climbed into my lap and started alternating between biting on my hand and making squealing noises, I was not surprised. Although the biting was slightly painful, the reactions from the passengers behind us to his squealing noises were much more painful.

By the time I felt the tap on my shoulder, I already knew this particular flight was not full of forgiving passengers. We had been fortunate on past flights to have had kindness, but today was not one of those days.

The tap on the shoulder was followed with "Is he going to keep making that noise for the whole flight? It is really starting to annoy some of us."

"I'm so sorry." I summoned up as much strength as I could spare to placate my fellow traveler. "Billy has autism. Please know that he is doing the best he can." I handed Billy a new toy, a distraction that would be short lived.

I could tell by the way her face dropped that the woman felt bad, but the grumbling from others seated behind us continued. I can take the looks of disgust from one or two people a day, but an entire flight of passengers for hours is too much.

Since we were in the bulkhead seats, just behind first class, I figured why not just address the entire flight and get it over with.

I set Billy in his seat, stood up, and faced the passengers. "Look, I'm sorry you have to deal with this for the next three hours. It's called autism, and we . . ." I pointed to my husband, Riley, and Billy. ". . . do this twenty-four hours a day, seven days a week." Then I plopped back into my seat, pulled Billy onto my lap, and quietly sobbed.

I would like to say that after I addressed the passengers, everyone was kind. Unfortunately, they were not, but the flight attendants and a few passengers went over and above to help us, and that made all the difference.

In fact, I will always be grateful for the handful of people who pop into our lives, probably not even knowing it's autism we're dealing with, but they know it's something. So when they see an eight-year-old sitting in the large part of the shopping cart while the groceries are being placed under the cart, they smile instead of judging. The kindness is so helpful. What they don't know is that I had to spend twenty minutes driving around the parking lot waiting for a spot right near the cart return to open up so I could park there, grab a cart, and wheel it up to the van to help Billy climb in.

It is nearly impossible for me to hoist a ninety-pound boy into a shopping cart, and without the security of riding in the cart, shopping is impossible for him. They also would not have known that Billy's limited tolerance for fluorescent lighting and the sensory overwhelm with all the smells, people, and noises only allows us fifteen minutes to get in and out of the store.

Our first stop is always for bananas. I grab ten, knowing that Billy will finish four or five before we make it to the checkout. At the checkout, I ask the clerk to weigh the remaining bananas and charge me double. Her understanding smile, instead of judgmental comments or looks, makes life so much better.

In all fairness, I must add that I can only hope I would be one of the smilers and not the judgers, but I will never know for sure how I would have reacted to the autism world if I didn't live in it.

CHAPTER 26

Matters of the Heart

JEFF

A phone call from a nurse at Children's Hospital causes a surge of mixed emotions in me.

"We now have a genetic test to determine whether Jessica or Colin has long QT syndrome," she says.

The heart condition that caused Charmaine's death.

I'm still at work, and I sink into my desk chair. Children's Hospital has been following Jessica for six years now, ever since her EKG first showed abnormalities when she was eight months old.

"Thank you for calling," I manage to say. "I will need to get back to you on that."

After hanging up, I call Nancy, who has become my most supportive and understanding friend. We talk through the pros and cons of knowing. If the test comes back inconclusive, we cannot rule out long QT anyway. However, if it comes back genetically positive for long QT, then they will start her on medication and a protocol to give her the best chance to live a long life. A part of me knows I need to have Jessica tested, but another part of me cannot stand the finality of knowing she has long QT—which cannot be cured.

"Jeff, I've been through some hard things with my Billy." Nancy's voice has a way of soothing me. "I know how difficult this is for you. If you want to get Jessica tested, I'd be happy to go with you."

Those words lift a huge weight off me. I have become used to taking Jessica for medical appointments by myself, and the thought of not being alone is comforting.

I'm still getting used to my recent revelation regarding my feelings for her and waiting for the right opportunity to tell her. Now, this new concern about Jessica makes waiting a little longer seem wise. I want the moment to feel just right.

The next week, as we head to Children's Hospital, Nancy turns around in her seat to face Jessica. "So, did your dad tell you what we are doing today?"

"Yes." Jessica nods matter-of-factly. "He said I'm taking a test."

"That's right, but it will be a little different than the tests you take at school."

Jessica huffs out a chuckle, and I catch a glimpse of her in the rearview mirror, rolling her eyes.

"That's good," she says. "I hate tests."

"Me too!" Nancy tosses me a glance that lets me know she's got this.

With her being a teacher, I know she can break the explanation down into simple terms for Jessica to understand.

Her focus returns to Jessica. "What tests do you take at school?"

"Spelling and math."

"And then you get a grade to tell you how well you did, right?"

Jessica nods, and Nancy continues.

"This test today will show us how your heart is doing. You won't get a grade, but the doctor will be able to tell if you need some medicine to help your heart work better."

"Okay."

Jessica's lack of apprehension makes me want to cry. Thank goodness Nancy is with us.

"After we are all done today, if it's all right with your dad . . ." She gives my arm a playful nudge. ". . . we can go get some ice cream. How does that sound?"

"Good! I want chocolate with sprinkles."

Seeing her make eye contact with me in the mirror, I smile. "You got it, Jessica."

When we arrive in the waiting room, Nancy pulls out a coloring book and crayons, and I watch as she and Jessica color pictures. When Jessica tires of coloring, Nancy reaches into her bag and pulls out a book of dot-to-dot pictures and some snacks.

I am so grateful not to be doing this alone, and I can hardly believe Nancy wants to help and how much she jumps in to comfort Jessica the way a mom would.

When they call Jessica's name, the three of us walk back for the blood draw.

The nurse asks Jessica to sit in the chair, places a band around her arm, and immediately sticks the needle in.

Jessica screams.

The nurse must have assumed Jessica knew the process, so she hadn't explained anything. I'm standing there shocked, but Nancy jumps in quickly and hugs Jessica to help hold her still and keep her calm.

Afterward, Jessica keeps looking at her Band-Aid.

"That's a cute little doggy Band-Aid," Nancy says. "You've been so brave, Jessica. Your dad and I are proud of you. You deserve some ice cream!"

"Ice cream, ice cream." Jessica tugs on Nancy's and my hands, urging us toward the door.

An hour later, as we are leaving the ice cream parlor, I turn to Nancy. "Well, going for ice cream was fun, but I think you and I should have a reward also. Why don't I take you out for dinner Friday night as a thank-you."

She glances at me, eyes shining. "That would be great. I agree that we deserve more than ice cream after the past couple of weeks. An IEP meeting and genetic testing should be worth some sushi and a martini." She smiles at me.

My heart is full.

On Friday night, I drop Jessica and Colin off at Nancy's house with the sitter, and we drive to our favorite restaurant—Roy's.

We have a great time at dinner, talking, laughing, and people watching. It feels like old times—back when we were dating. I open my mouth more than once intending to tell her I've changed my mind, but I hold back. I don't want her to think that my sole motivation is wanting help with my kids. And besides, I still haven't figured out how to break the news to the kids' grandparents.

We return to Nancy's house after our dinner out. Our kids, as always, have had a fun evening together.

As the sitter is leaving, she turns and casually mentions to Nancy, "I almost forgot. Someone named Jason called."

I can't help shooting a questioning look at Nancy, but her pleasant smile seems frozen. My stomach drops. Is this the guy she was out on the town with while I sat home with my kids watching *Toy Story*?

For a split second, I consider making a lame joke about it, but I decide it's better to ignore it and hope that everyone else does too.

But then Jessica asks Riley, "Who's Jason?"

Nancy's mouth starts to twitch, and she sends me a look that seems to be saying "I'm sorry!"

"He's really fun!" Riley jumps up and down with excitement. "He comes over, and we play board games!"

I say nothing beyond some quick encouragement to Colin and Jessica to get their things and head to the car.

Once I've pulled into our garage, Colin grabs my housekey, and he and Jessica jump out of the car and race into the house. Although I tuned out most of their argument on the way home, I know it was about Jessica wanting to watch *Care Bears* when we get home. I'm still in the garage, but I can hear Jessica yelling.

"Colin, I said I was going to watch *Care Bears*. Colin! Dad, Dad! It's not fair!"

I stay in the garage, just sitting in the car, thinking about that phone call Nancy received. Who is this Jason guy? Mr. Fun-and-Board-Games. Nancy never mentioned him, but it's clear from hearing Riley and her excitement that he may be someone Nancy is pretty interested in. She has told me before that she doesn't let just anyone meet her kids, so this means she's had more than a couple of dates with him. She might be getting serious about him.

I actually feel my forehead start to sweat. Maybe she is seeing a possible future with someone other than me. Then I remember, she isn't seeing a future with me. I'm the one who told her there is no future with me. I have to tell her I've reconsidered and pray I'm not too late.

I go into the house and see Colin and Jessica arguing about the remote control.

"Colin, come on. Let her watch *Care Bears* first. She has to go to bed soon."

I then go about the routine of getting the laundry put away and cleaning the kitchen, but my mind continues to drift back to that phone call. I do not want to lose her, this much I know.

It feels like it takes forever to get the kids to bed. I look at the clock next to my bed. It's not too late to call Nancy. Sure, maybe this isn't the ideal, romantic moment I've been waiting for. But I might have waited too long as it is.

I move for the phone, but the blinking light on the answering machine distracts me. Maybe Nancy left me a message, wanting to apologize for not telling me about Jason.

But the voice on the message isn't Nancy. It's the doctor from Children's Hospital. The test results have come back sooner than I might have preferred.

Jessica *does* have long QT. She will have to go on medication, and I will need to carry an automated external defibrillator everywhere I go, since regular CPR won't be enough to bring her back if she has an event.

I sit on the end of the bed, shaken, and not sure I can handle one more disappointment tonight. My call to Nancy can wait.

Life is full of ups and downs.

CHAPTER 27

Not-So-Silly Rule

NANCY

The next few weeks are very busy with play rehearsal for Riley and being there for Jeff as he adjusts to Jessica's diagnosis. Jason, whom I had started dating and actually feel hopeful that I might have a future with, calls me a few times, but we have a hard time syncing our schedules.

Although Jeff and I text and talk often, we don't find time to get together. I'm surprised when he calls on a Tuesday afternoon and asks if he can come over.

"I only have an hour before Billy's bus gets here." My stomach clenches a little. It's such an odd time for us to get together. "I think it will work, though. Is everything okay?"

"Yes," he says. "I just want to see you."

"Okay," I say, not quite sure what to make of that. "See you soon."

When he arrives, we sit on the sofa in the living room. Something feels off.

"Are you sure everything's okay?" I ask him again.

In the next instant, he is on a knee in front of me with a ring in his hand. "Will you marry me?"

I'm practically speechless. I did not see this coming. My heart pounds as I stare at the square diamond set in white gold. I want to say yes, but I'm frankly too stunned.

Finally, I stammer, "R-really? Is this for real?" "Yes." He gives me a shaky smile. "This is real."

"You want to marry me?"

He nods sincerely. "I want our families to be a family."

That is exactly what I need to hear. "Well then, yes! I want that too!"

In one swift motion, he slips the ring onto my finger and shifts back to the sofa, then wraps me in his arms.

But I'm still in a state of shock. "You really want this?" I say again. It's hard to believe, because Jeff has always said he *might* get married again after his kids are grown. They're still only eleven and seven.

I'm so caught off guard that poor Jeff has to assure me several times. But I'm also excited!

We decide not to tell the kids about our decision until we've sorted everything out. They think we are just friends who attend some meetings together—they have no idea how much we've come to count on each other. Though clearly, Jessica thinks it's a good idea—for a couple of months now, she has been saying, "You and my dad should get married so Riley and I can be sisters!"

On Friday when Jeff and I go out for dinner, I wear my ring. Otherwise, when the kids are around, I keep it safely tucked away in a drawer.

Over dinner, I suggest that when school is out in a few weeks, we should rent a cabin in the mountains for a weekend to see what it's like for all of us to spend time together. We've spent Sunday afternoons together, and we've been to the circus and Disneyland, but we have not had all six of us in one place for more than a few hours.

We also decide to find a Christian counselor who specializes in blended families. I take an old receipt and a pen from my purse, and we make a list of all the issues we need to figure out.

It is quite a list, but we want to be careful about our decision:

- Where will we live?
- What school will the kids attend? (At this point, they are in four different schools.)
- How will we blend parenting styles?

- What will the house rules be?
- What discipline methods will we use?
- What do we have to consider for Billy's long-term needs?
- What types of meals will we eat? (Jeff is more junk-food dad, while I am healthy-food mom.)
- Is this a good idea for our kids too, or just for us?
- What church will we attend? Since my church is out of the question now, maybe Jeff's church?

At our first few meetings with Sherry, our counselor, we focus on parenting styles. One of my concerns is that Jeff is a lot more structured in some ways than I am, and Billy and Riley are not used to that.

"For example," I say to our therapist, "even though we have a playroom, I also allow toys to be played with all over the house. It isn't unusual to have a tower of stuffed animals on the couch in the living room. Or for toys to line the tile walkway between the living room and the kitchen."

I take a breath, wanting to feel understood. "If Riley has a game going, like with her Littlest Pet Shop toys, she'll often leave it set up for days." I motion to my fiancé. "Jeff, on the other hand, likes toys cleaned up after they are played with and doesn't really understand that if the pretend play game is ongoing, those pet shops need to stay exactly where they are until play resumes the next day."

I express concerns about Jeff wanting kids dressed before they come downstairs in the morning. On school days, I am in complete agreement, but weekends at our house are different. It is not at all unusual for Riley to play all morning on a Saturday while still wearing her pajamas.

I share with the therapist a conversation Jeff and I had one Saturday when he came to pick up Jessica from sleeping over. It was after lunch, and Jessica and Riley were still in their pajamas. They had been playing all morning with their Pet Shop toys and just couldn't be bothered with getting dressed.

When Jeff walked in, the first thing he said was "Why aren't they dressed?"

"They are playing," I responded.

"They should be dressed. It's already twelve thirty in the afternoon."

"It's Saturday, and they have been having fun all morning. What's the big deal?" I keep my tone lighthearted.

"I just think they should get dressed first thing in the morning and then play."

"Well, that rarely happens here on the weekends," I tell him. "They are just having fun."

Sherry asks Jeff why it's important to him.

"I don't really know," he replies. "I just know that it is."

This issue will stay on the list for sure, as I'm not on board for requiring that change. It's just too structured and will suck some of the joy out of childhood.

By the time we leave our first counseling session, we have covered a lot of ground.

But the following Saturday morning, when Jeff comes to pick Jessica up, she is still in her pajamas, and I can tell he's working hard to bite his tongue. I give him a hug and whisper, "It's okay—it really is."

The next Friday night as we leave my house to go to dinner, I slip my engagement ring onto my finger. It is so great to wear it! While dining at our table in our favorite restaurant, Roy's, we alternate between people watching and planning the menu for our weekend trip with the kids, which is only a week away.

When we head to the car later, hand in hand, Jeff asks, "While we are at the cabin, can we have a rule that the kids get dressed before coming downstairs for breakfast?"

I consider, then ask lightly, "Why do you think it's such a big deal to you?"

"I just remember"—he takes a deep breath before continuing—"the morning Charmaine passed away." He squeezes my hand.

"Colin was downstairs in his pajamas. She always had him get dressed first thing, but that day when I came home for lunch, he was standing there in his pajamas."

"Oh my gosh!" I stop midstride and turn toward him. "That's it! It's a PTSD thing for you." I give him a long hug.

I get it now. It isn't just a silly rule—it's to avoid having a flashback to the day his wife died.

I have my PTSD too. Just setting foot in a hospital takes me right back to the day my husband barely survived surgery. I even remember the smell of the hand soap the hospital used. To this day, if I get a whiff of that scent, I'm immediately right back in that place.

But I still can't agree to his now not-so-silly rule. We'll have to keep working on that one.

CHAPTER 28

Does God Care About the Little Things?

NANCY

On a Monday morning, I pull into the church parking lot, grab my Bible and coffee, and head into Bible study. I've learned so much in this group, and the women are some of the kindest people I've ever met.

I have even been fortunate to meet another autism mom, Gia. Although our challenges in caring for our boys do not allow us to get together often, when we do meet outside of the group for coffee or breakfast, I can tell that I have met a lifelong friend.

Thanks to this group, I understand much more about God than I ever thought I would, and I have my favorite Bible verses, but still.

I have a tendency to be impatient. When there's a task I want to accomplish, I'm good about coming up with the quickest solution. But while finishing my homework on Sunday nights, I begin to realize that Bible fluency will not be quickly accomplished and checked off my list. In fact, I need to slow down, take a deep breath, and settle in for a lifetime.

But what I can't seem to wrap my head around is the idea of having a personal relationship with Jesus. I do accept the gift of eternity with Him, and I know that it's a gift and not something I earn through trying to be perfect, because of these two verses:

For God so loved the world, that he gave his only begotten Son, that whosoever believeth in him should not perish, but have everlasting life. (John 3:16)

For it is by grace you have been saved, through faith— and this is not from yourselves, it is the gift of God—not by works, so that no one can boast. (Ephesians 2:8–9)

The more I learn about the life, death, and resurrection of Jesus, the more everything makes sense.

Yet each week as we share our prayer requests, several women ask for prayer for seemingly minor things. I only ever pray for really big things or life-and-death situations—my mom's cancer; when I left Keith—and then I hope that God answers. Many of the women ask God for things that I would never consider asking—for a job interview, help buying a house, to sort out finances. I struggle to believe He has time for the little things, and I don't believe He cares much about my minor problems. *Don't they realize God is busy running the world and isn't concerned with their job or where they live?*

But if I have a relationship with Him, wouldn't that mean He does care? He loves me, right?

It's hard to undo my childhood religious training. I was led to believe that God was super disappointed with me for not doing better, for not doing more, and for failing to perfectly jump through all the religious hoops set in front of me. As long as I hold on to the belief that He is disappointed in me, I am not likely to have a close relationship with Him.

I do know that during my toughest times, when I turn to Him in prayer, He gives me peace, and this verse describes that peace: "Peace I leave with you; my peace I give you. I do not give to you as the world gives. Do not let your hearts be troubled and do not be afraid" (John 14:27). I know firsthand the peace from Him that has washed over me during some really tough times. It's not peace from this world.

After leaving my study on Monday, I wrestle with this issue of a personal relationship. If I can really have it, I want it.

A few days later, I turn to the internet because I tend to feel I'm bothering people if I ask too many questions. I find the answer to my question on Gotquestions.org:

> Question: What does it mean to have a personal relationship with God?

> Answer: The Holy Spirit has been given to us as our Counselor. Jesus said this before He died, and after He died, the Holy Spirit became available to all who earnestly seek to receive Him. He is the one who lives in the hearts of believers and never leaves. He counsels us, teaches us truths, and changes our hearts. Without this divine Holy Spirit, we would not have the ability to fight against evil and temptations. But since we do have Him, we begin to produce the fruit that comes from allowing the Spirit to control us: love, joy, peace, patience, kindness, goodness, faithfulness, gentleness, and self-control.[1]

There is another thing I find absolutely confusing. Although I know Jesus is the Son of God, I am really struggling to understand what they call "the Trinity." It just seems complicated. Do I pray to God? To Jesus? I know the Holy Spirit is God's Spirit in us when we become believers in what Jesus did for us, but how does it all fit together?

I'm very relieved at the answer I find on Gotquestions.org:

> The most difficult thing about the Christian concept of the Trinity is that there is no way to perfectly and completely understand it. The Trinity is a concept that

---

1   Got Questions, https://www.gotquestions.org/personal-relationship-with-God.html.

is impossible for any human being to fully understand, let alone explain. God is infinitely greater than we are; therefore, we should not expect to be able to fully understand Him. The Bible teaches that the Father is God, that Jesus is God, and that the Holy Spirit is God. The Bible also teaches that there is only one God. Though we can understand some facts about the relationship of the different Persons of the Trinity to one another, ultimately, it is incomprehensible to the human mind. However, this does not mean the Trinity is not true or that it is not based on the teachings of the Bible.[2]

Now it all makes sense. It's not me working hard for love, joy, peace, patience, kindness, goodness, faithfulness, gentleness, and self-control (fruit of the Spirit)—it's me inviting and allowing the Holy Spirit (God's Spirit, promised to believers) to provide the fruit of the Spirit for me, as He chooses. I'd thought it was up to me to get myself together enough for God, and it's really the other way around—letting God get me together.

My problem, though, is that I still want God to answer my prayers the way I see fit. I want to ask for something and have it done. Now. When my prayers are not answered the way I want, I decide that God must not care about me as much as I'd like.

But I'm making strides with trusting Him with the little things, and I pray for our upcoming weekend trip with the kiddos.

---

2   Got Questions, https://www.gotquestions.org/Trinity-Bible.html.

CHAPTER 29

Cabin Adventure

JEFF

We arrive at the cabin just as the sun dips behind the treetops, leaving cottony streaks of orange and red and purple. I park Nancy's van in the driveway. It's on a slight incline, so when I open the back, several bags of food topple out. I look at the food, then at Nancy and the kids, then back to the food, with what I hope is a comical, dazed expression.

We all laugh and then scramble to grab stuff before it rolls away. Inside, there's a bedroom downstairs for Colin and me, and a bedroom upstairs for Nancy and Billy. The girls get to sleep in the loft, which ramps up their excitement.

While the girls lug their backpacks to the loft, Nancy boils some water to make a big pot of spaghetti. Within an hour, we sit down at the table for dinner.

When Colin gags on the spaghetti and complains that his stomach hurts, I get the impression he's less than excited to be on this getaway. He's sometimes a little dramatic, but this is the first time it seems directed at Nancy. This might be a long weekend!

Billy hangs out in the downstairs bedroom, which is near the kitchen, with his portable DVD player. Nancy assures me that he often needs breaks from being around so many people.

But I'm uneasy, and I need to say something.

"Hey," I say as I help Nancy clear the table. "I've unpacked our stuff in that room. I have my contact lens case on the dresser. Billy won't mess with it, will he?"

She appears unconcerned. "Billy has never touched my contact lenses, and he knows right where I keep them." She sets a stack of plates on the counter. "He'll just watch his DVD player."

Later that night, we search the floor for my contacts.

The next day after breakfast, we play some board games while Billy watches movies. Jessica whines about Colin's feet being too close to her. When she pushes his feet away, Colin complains she's hitting him.

I look at Riley at the start of a game and say, "You're going down," which leads Riley to run upstairs crying.

Sigh.

In the afternoon, Billy wants to watch TV, and Colin attempts to help him with the remote control—which Billy misunderstands. In frustration, he throws the remote across the room.

That evening, while Nancy is settling Billy into bed and I'm watching TV, Riley climbs down from the loft complaining that the TV is too loud. Jessica comes downstairs a few minutes later crying because she forgot her teddy bear.

After we finally get all the kids settled for the evening, Nancy and I head out to the front porch.

"Taking care of four kids sure isn't the same as two kids," Nancy says as she plops onto an Adirondack chair.

"You can say that again." I laugh as I sit in the other chair. I drum my fingertips on the table between us.

The next morning, we are more than ready to pack up and leave. A few hours later, it is a huge relief when we pull into Nancy's driveway. My kids and I follow Nancy and her kids into their house. As her kids trudge to their rooms, I give Nancy a quick hug.

"It's so good to be home," she says.

I hug her tighter, nodding.

Over the next few weeks, we meet with the counselor and work on our list. The problem is, there are so many complicated elements. Nancy mentions that she's begun to appreciate my initial thought about waiting to remarry until my kids are grown. She admits to seeing the sense in that and that she's having doubts whether getting married is a good idea.

We have two big issues we just can't resolve:

Letting the kids have their toys in the main areas of the house. If they have an ongoing game on the weekends, letting them keep it all set up. With Nancy's background (special ed teacher), she knows the importance of pretend play, which she encourages. I, on the other hand, want everything cleaned up at the end of the day.

My parents and my in-laws (Charmaine's parents) are involved in the day-to-day with Colin and Jessica. I'm not sure how to continue to allow them that same level of interaction after we get married. This is especially hard because neither of the grandmothers wants me to remarry. They are not going to be supportive.

Before going into our next counseling session, while we're still in the parking lot, Nancy says, "You know, Jeff, there just might be some things on our list that we can't resolve. Maybe it really is too much, and we're trying to force this to work when it's not meant to be."

"I agree." Relief floods over me as I come to a stop and face her. "It's hard with my parents. It's hard with Charmaine's parents. They're all going to be upset. It's probably for the best if we just keep things like they are now."

She slips her engagement ring off her finger and gives it to me. Reluctantly, I put it in my pocket and blink back some tears.

Why does life have to be so complicated?

CHAPTER 30

Praying Together

NANCY

I spend the next week feeling sad and disappointed. If we didn't have issues with the kids and in-laws, Jeff would be perfect for me. As a problem solver, it's tough to face issues I can't solve. But since we enjoy our time together and Jessica and Riley are good friends, we continue to see each other as we shuttle them back and forth.

It's still hard to wrap my head around it all, and I agree to go to dinner with Tracey one Friday night to talk it through.

We dine in a little restaurant on the coast. I always have a great time with her, and she is also an autism mom, so she understands my challenges. She is surprised that Jeff and I even considered trying to blend our families.

"I like Jeff, but it seems like it's way too much to consider." She passes the basket of bread my way.

"You're right." Hating to admit it, I take out my frustration on a piece of bread by slathering it with way too much butter. "With four kids—and one who has a pretty significant disability—it's too complicated. We couldn't even agree on some of the little things—let alone the big ones."

But still, the sadness continually seeps back in.

An ache hits my heart every time I see Jeff. Our two girls are still best friends, and he swings by often to drop Jessica off and pick her up.

Jeff and I still feel the same way about each other—we just can't figure out how to make it all work.

Making it even harder for me to let go, on Sundays Billy, Riley, and I spend time at Jeff's, barbequing and swimming. Though I have to give up the dream of being one family, I do find consolation in having a great friend.

One Sunday after we get home, I'm particularly lonely, and I log in to the dating website to scroll through the profiles or to see who has emailed me. I've done this a few times, as I'm considering dating again. But the more I think about it, the more I cannot imagine meeting someone I like more than Jeff. However, since I don't have a future with him, I feel like I need to start dating again. It feels like it'll be a lot of work.

Nancy, I tell myself, *you're still so involved with Jeff and his kids. Maybe you should wait till there's less going on with the two of you.*

That seems unlikely, though, since our activities continue to involve all the kids.

School's out for the summer, so I enroll Riley and Jessica in an art class. Once a month on Friday evenings, Jeff and I take the kids to the summer concert at the park. We pack a picnic basket and blanket and spend time relaxing and listening to music.

We get each other, and the fact that our senses of humor are so similar is an added bonus. We have fun when we're together.

One night while Jeff and I are talking on the phone, I mention that my Bible study that day focused on the power of prayer.

"How would you feel about praying together on the phone every night?" I ask hesitantly. "We could put our whole relationship situation in God's hands and then trust Him to work it out if it's meant to be. If it's not meant to be, He will make that really clear also."

"I could get on board for that," Jeff replies.

For the next several weeks, we begin our prayer time with a simple prayer: "Lord, we thank You for all the times You have directed our paths and given us peace during really tough circumstances. We are asking now that if it is Your will that we become one family, You will make it really clear to us. We pray this in Jesus's name, Amen."

Praying out loud with someone is still new to me; the memorized prayers I recited while growing up don't count. Fortunately, I've heard many prayers being said aloud during my Bible study, so I have a general idea of what to say. But the first few times we pray, I feel awkward.

After we've prayed together for a few weeks, I'm doing my Bible study homework one evening. I come across a reassuring passage in *The Jeremiah Study Bible*, with notes by Dr. David Jeremiah:

> He knows instantly when we are genuinely seeking Him or when we are just going through the motions. The fact is, He does not desire our traditions, our giving, even our prayer and Bible reading . . . unless these things come from an obedient, truly loving heart. If our external actions toward God do not flow from an authentic desire to love others and please Him, we are only putting on a religious show and He wants none of it.[3]

I find it reassuring that praying isn't about the right words or the proper structure—it's the realness of it and whether I am in good standing (nothing unconfessed) with the One who hears and answers.

A couple of months later, while we're talking on the phone about our plans for Christmas, Jeff says, "You know, I really have complete peace about us getting married."

"You do?" I swallow hard before adding, "It's strange, but I do too."

We haven't worked out any of the things that were on that list, but I have peace.

---

3   David Jeremiah, *The Jeremiah Study Bible* (Franklin, Tennessee: Worthy Books, 2013). 1,176.

The next morning, we meet for coffee and look at the list we created. Neither one of us can even figure out why we thought all those things were such a big deal.

Friday night, while all the kids are at my house with the sitter, Jeff takes me out to dinner at Roy's. While we're waiting for our food, he stands and then kneels on one knee beside me, holding a ring box.

Oh my.

"Nancy, my love for you is deeper than any problems that might arise. I believe God has brought us together, and I want to honor that. Will you marry me? No going back this time!"

I throw my arms around him. "Yes!"

This time, I don't ask him if he "really" wants to get married. Jeff had already returned the ring he'd given me before, so I slip on an all-new diamond.

The employees, who know us pretty well by now, pop the champagne and congratulate us.

After dinner, as we drive to Jeff's house to figure out which room will be Riley's and which room will be Billy's, he says he wants to play a song for me.

I hear the first notes of "I Will Be Here," by Steven Curtis Chapman, and tears immediately push at the backs of my eyes. "How did you know about this song?"

"Know *what* about it?" He casts me a puzzled glance. "I just like this song."

I'm barely able to get out the words as tears create rivers to my chin. "This is the song I used to listen to years ago, and I'd think, if I ever start dating, this is the kind of man I'm going to look for."

He pulls the car to the side of the road and gives me a hug.

This is going to be a huge change, but at least I know how to prepare Billy for changes. In the autism world, there is something called "social stories." Anytime something in Billy's life is going to change, I write a book and add pictures to it. Then we read it over and over, so when the change or event happens, he is prepared.

We aren't concerned with how Riley and Jessica, who are nine and seven now, will take the news—they'll be thrilled—but we're not sure Colin will be happy. Of course, we aren't sure he'll be unhappy either. He doesn't like change, and he doesn't know we're dating, so he'll be surprised.

On Monday, I call to schedule an appointment with our counselor. We want to share the good news and enlist her help with telling Colin.

Our counselor, Sherry, assures us that even if Colin doesn't embrace the idea, it will be for his good to have both a mother and father. Since he is only eleven years old (the same age as Billy), the idea of a big change might cause anxiety, but in the long run, this marriage will benefit all our kids.

The following Friday night, we take Colin out for burgers at Coco's. After we are seated in our booth and have placed our order, we make small talk for a while to ease into our reason for being there. Finally, we look at each other, then at Colin.

"So." Jeff sits forward, striking that balance between casual and celebratory. "We have some big news."

Colin smiles, showing his mouthful of braces. "Okay."

"Well, Nancy and I have known each other for a while now, and we've decided to get married. This will mean that we will all become one family."

At that moment, the server shows up with our hamburgers, so we pause our conversation.

After Colin takes a couple of bites of his burger, Jeff asks, "So, what do you think?"

Lifting a shoulder, he says, "I think that's good," then takes a sip of his soda.

I'm surprised, but I try not to show it. We finish our meal while talking about school and friends. The dinner feels like a success, but I can tell by the unease in Jeff's expression that he shares my concern that Colin doesn't have much to say about our big announcement.

After dinner, we drop Colin off at home—he's old enough to be there by himself for a short time—before heading to my house to tell the girls.

The sitter leaves, and we gather the girls in the living room.

"We have some big news." I sit forward, my fingers weaving together in my lap. "Do you want to guess?"

Jessica's face lights up. "We are going to Disneyland!"

I shake my head. "Nope."

"You're getting married." Riley adds a little laugh that's hard to decipher.

"Yes, we are." I smile at Jeff.

"What?" Riley's expression narrows. "Are you *really?*"

"Yes, we really are!"

Riley folds her arms and looks skeptical. Since I play a lot of practical jokes, she must think this is one of them.

"Really," I insist. "We are!"

Jessica giggles and falls to the floor, then rolls around. She is so excited.

It takes a few minutes to convince Riley, but when she finally believes us, she joins Jessica in her glee.

"We are going to be sisters!" They chant in unison as they jump up and down. "We are going to be sisters!"

Jeff slips his hand over mine, and we relish the sweet moment. After we answer a million questions about how soon we can get married and how soon they can become sisters, Jeff heads to the door. Jessica is spending the night, so the girls can continue their celebration.

"Call me after you talk to Colin again," I whisper to him at the door.

A half an hour or so later, my phone rings. Seeing on the caller ID that it's Jeff, I escape to my room so the girls won't hear my conversation—even though they're preoccupied with their soon-to-be sisterhood.

"Hey." I'm a little out of breath from dashing up the stairs. "So how is Colin?"

"He's fine. However, his first question-slash-statement, when I asked if he was okay, was, 'So they'll live in their house, and we'll live in ours, right?'"

"That explains the lack of reaction." I pause. "Did you break the news that we'll be moving in?"

"Yes, and I think he's good with it."

"I hope so." *Even if he doesn't know it, this is still what's best for him,* I remind myself.

A few days later, my worries are put to rest. Jeff and Colin come over to pick Jessica up from a playdate, and as I'm coming out of the laundry room, Colin asks, "Are you going to become my evil stepmother?"

"Yes, I am." I chase him around the house, making scary evil-stepmother noises, much to Colin's delight.

Thank You, God, for giving us all peace.

CHAPTER 31

We Are a Family!

NANCY

Tuesday, June 1, 2010. I cannot believe this day is finally here. We're getting married on a Tuesday because that's part and parcel of planning a wedding a few months in advance; all the Saturdays at the church have been booked. It is midafternoon when we all pull into the church parking lot. My sister Juli helps the girls with their dresses and shoes before helping me with my hair and makeup.

Later, while I button Billy's suit coat and straighten his tie, Jeff and Colin head into the church. Colin, as the best man, is in charge of carrying the rings. Jeff would tell me later that as the elevator doors slid apart, Colin dropped the rings and stepped on them barely in time to keep them from falling down the elevator shaft. *Whew!*

Finally, it's time for the ceremony.

Standing in the foyer, I turn to look at the girls—they're so beautiful in their light-green dresses and white pearl headbands. When the sanctuary doors open for the girls to walk down the aisle, I gaze at the faces of all our friends and family. I see my friend Gia and her son, Sage, sitting in the second row. It feels like a dream come true. Although I liked the idea that I might one day meet someone to share my life with again, the feeling that it is actually happening fills my heart with joy.

As Billy walks me down the aisle, I whisper, "Thank You, God." Jeff smiles at us with such warmth and a sparkle in his eyes that banishes any nervousness I feel. I am excited for our future together as a couple and as a family.

After the ceremony, as we all climb into the minivan, we can feel the excitement. It's real—we are a family now. A family with a mom and a dad. We are so grateful.

Jeff and I drop the kids off at home (the kids and I had moved most of our belongings into Jeff's home a week before the wedding), and my sister watches them while Jeff and I celebrate with dinner out at a local restaurant.

We skip a honeymoon, of course, and are up the next day packing lunches and driving kids to school.

Over the next few weeks, we all adjust to life as a bigger family. Now that my family has gone from three people to six people, grocery shopping, cooking, and laundry have doubled. The kids attend three different schools, so working out the carpool logistics is no small task. Yet somehow, every evening when we all gather around the dinner table, we end up having a great time. Having a big family is such a blessing!

Whenever I'm out and about and have a conversation about the kids and someone asks, "How old are your kids?" I answer, "Eight, ten, twelve, and twelve."

The immediate response is, "Oh, twins!"

I explain that we are a blended family, a God-blended family. This leads to some great conversations about the history of our family. I am always excited to share the story of how God brought us together.

But God knows, it isn't all easy.

One of our biggest adjustments involves food. Although I think I'm being very strategic and somewhat subtle while removing junk food and replacing it with healthier options, there are times when I'm not so sure.

One night while I'm cooking dinner, Colin comes into the kitchen looking for a snack. From the pantry, he calls out, "Mom, do we have any more cheese crackers?"

Uh-oh. Busted.

"I think we may be out, Colin." I do my best to sound guiltless. "There are some pretzels on the lowest shelf on the right."

"Okay." He sounds a little disappointed. "What about SunnyD or Yoohoo?"

"We're out," I answer, knowing full well that earlier I threw two bottles in the trash. "How about some water?"

He emerges from the pantry, carrying the bag of pretzels and eyeing me with suspicion. But he fills a cup with water and seems accepting of his fate.

Since Riley grew up with me, she is very used to drinking water as her main beverage. She is also used to reading the ingredients before buying anything that's prepackaged. One day, I overhear her explaining good nutrition to Jessica. It makes me smile.

The other thing that makes me smile is hearing Riley, Jessica, and Colin argue over chores. Ordinarily, the sound of arguing is not good, but I find it heartwarming to know they are interacting like siblings.

When Riley says, "It's my turn to dry. You dried last time," Colin responds, "I washed last night, and you dried."

Jessica jumps in while clearing the table. "Colin, last night you dried."

"Oh, yeah." Colin remembers and agrees, and the three of them continue in getting the chores done.

It's a good sign that our families are blending well.

After they finish the dishes, all of us settle on the couch to watch an episode of *The Middle*. It is currently one of our favorite shows, and we end up watching three episodes before we call it a night. There's just something about this imperfect but loving family—middle age, middle class, middle America—that feels comfortable and familiar.

If life were a sitcom, I like to think that ours would be this entertaining.

CHAPTER 32

Road Trip 2010: Monterey

JEFF

A couple of months after the wedding, Nancy and I plan a new family adventure. A road trip.

We both have great memories of taking road trips during our childhoods, and we want our kids to make similar memories. We plan to visit my brother and sister-in-law in Northern California before heading over to Monterey to see the aquarium.

Nancy and I couldn't be more excited that our kids finally have a complete family. When the fall school assignment to write about "what you did over the summer" comes around, they will actually have something to write about.

The day before we leave, as Nancy prepares food and I get the car ready, Riley and Jessica go into the garage loaded down with stuffed animals.

Later, as I place the water bottles in each of the cup holders, I see that the back seat in the Suburban has been all organized. Riley and Jessica have lined up their favorite stuffed animals, their Fisher-Price cameras, and pillows and blankets. I love how excited they are for this trip.

The next morning at six, we load everyone into our old Suburban and head off on our nine-hour drive. We take little video segments in which Nancy asks the kids what they are most excited about. We sing songs and eat junk food—a special treat now that Nancy has eliminated it from our daily diet. We play Mad Libs, where each of the kids gives Nancy a noun, verb, or adjective, and then she reads the resulting silly story aloud.

One of our favorite activities during our visit with my brother and sister-in-law is going out on their boat.

As my brother speeds up, Billy smiles from ear to ear saying, "Faster!" while at the same time Nancy is saying, "No, not faster. Slower, please!"

My brother looks at me, and we both shrug.

In the end, we all have a great time.

In Monterey, we visit the aquarium and walk around town. We eat dinner at a Mexican restaurant that has a mechanical bull. We decide it looks like fun. Nancy rides first, and thankfully, the ride operator is kind enough to slow it down, which helps. But Nancy still ends up on the mat much quicker than she'd like.

I go next, assuming an unfortunate let-me-show-you-how-it's-done swagger. Within seconds, the ride operator shows *me* how it's done by speeding it up. So much for my imagined career as a rodeo rider.

As Colin climbs onto the bull, I reach for Nancy's hand and say, "It's so much more fun going on vacation as a family rather than a single parent."

She squeezes my hand in agreement, and we cheer Colin on to near-victory.

Next, we watch as Riley takes her turn. She starts out looking good since she's been riding horses, and she's a dancer with very good balance.

After a minute, the operator seems to realize that in order to throw her, he will have to speed it up. It makes me nervous as I watch her going faster and faster. I can tell she's having a great time, and she manages to stay on till her ride comes to an abrupt end.

She stays by the bull, helping Billy climb on. What a great sister she is. I watch as Nancy quickly walks over to the operator. I can't hear what she's telling him, but I know she's explaining Billy's situation. He nods and seems to find just the right pace for Billy—fun, but not too fast.

Billy smiles big, clearly enjoying himself. I keep expecting him to yell out, "Faster!" but he seems perfectly content with the level the operator keeps him at.

Jessica is a little reluctant but also doesn't want to be left out. She climbs on and rides slowly—thank you, ride operator—until she gently slides to the side and falls to the mat, giggling like the little girl that she is.

The last morning of our vacation, we stop at a coffee shop before leaving for our nine-hour drive back home. After breakfast, we pile back into the Suburban. I start the engine, and we hear a loud *squeal*, then silence. The car refuses to start.

I groan.

"What do you think that means?" Nancy gives me a look that says she thinks I know more than I do about auto mechanics.

"I'm not sure," I say truthfully, "but it sounds like a broken fan belt."

It's always tough when your car breaks down, especially far from home, but for us, having two adults to handle the situation makes it seem like less of a big deal.

After a phone call and a brief wait, Nancy heads across the parking lot to a bookstore with the four kids while I drive off with the tow truck driver.

Later, I call Nancy to tell her it's more than just the fan belt, and it will take several days to fix the car.

She groans. Then I hear a little chuckle that makes me wonder if my wife has finally lost it.

"You know," she says, "if this were an episode of *The Middle*, it would be hilarious."

I laugh too. "That's a good way to see it. Our own little sitcom."

Since all the hotels in town are full, we make a quick decision to rent a car for the rest of the drive home. I will bring it back in a few days to pick up our good-as-new Suburban. We then spend several hours trying to locate a rental car that can seat six.

By the time we finally start our long drive home, it's late afternoon. We're tired, and so are the kids, but I can't help smiling as I clutch Nancy's hand. I feel so grateful for something I will never take for granted—having a partner to share life with, whether in good times or bad.

CHAPTER 33

Expanding Trust

NANCY

Another year has passed, and it's summer again.

Riley and Jessica are in the pool laughing and having a fun time, and I'm in the kitchen baking muffins. I hope to have them out of the oven before Billy's bus arrives. The girls and Colin are on summer break, but since Billy has an autism diagnosis, he qualifies for year-round school.

Every morning at 7:40, the bus pulls up to the curb in front of our house. At 12:40 p.m., the bus brings him home. If I leave the front windows open, I can usually hear it approaching from the kitchen. Billy must have someone meet him at the bus, and most days that someone is me.

The KitchenAid mixer is going full speed. As I measure out the final ingredient, I look through the window again to see the girls doing underwater handstands, then climbing onto the rafts while laughing about something. Just as I pour the baking soda into the mix and watch it being blended in, I realize I added corn starch by mistake. I turn the mixer off, wondering if the batter can be salvaged. But there's no way to undo the mistake. I have to throw it out and start over.

Although I'm frustrated, I also recognize that this setback is really nothing in the big picture. It also occurs to me that this is similar to many things in life. I can have 90 percent of the right ingredients, but that one wrong ingredient can really mess it all up.

I ponder again about my religious beliefs from my childhood and how they can still catch me off guard and interfere with the truth—that God loves me and hears my prayers.

While growing up, the focus was on perfect behavior. I never heard about God loving me. My parents didn't say *I love you*, and they weren't concerned with or involved in my day-to-day life. Don't get me wrong; they provided for me. I never had to worry about having food or clothing, but they did not express any interest in what I was up to. That translated to my child-brain as them not loving me.

It's hard to let go of these ingrained lies. I realize that unless I fully remove those false religious ingredients, I'll continue to struggle with fully accepting the truth.

As I scoop out the flour to restart the muffin recipe, I also recognize that I must be strong and determined to replace the old religious falsehoods with the truth. Kind of like breaking a bad habit—replace it with a good habit. To do this, I know I need to fully identify the false beliefs I have and replace them with truths from Scripture.

When blending the dry ingredients, I recall a time in my early twenties when I worked as a bank teller. We tellers were trained in how to recognize counterfeit money. Although we had several samples of good counterfeits, we mostly studied the details of the real thing so we would recognize the sometimes-subtle differences in the counterfeit.

The same is true with God's Word versus false teachings.

A short while later, as I'm removing the pans from the oven, I hear Billy's bus coming. I wipe my hands on a towel and hurry to the front door.

Standing in the doorway as Billy's bus approaches the curb, I make a mental note to myself that unless I really study the Bible and know it well, I probably won't recognize a good counterfeit belief.

I once believed the lie that there is a long list of things I must do if I want any chance of getting into heaven one day. That is simply not true. Once Jesus died for us and then rose from the dead, He had paid the price for us. He promises eternal life to all who accept this gift from Him. I have accepted this gift and now live with the assurance of being with Him. There is nothing more I have to do, other than learn His Word and live life the way He wants me to. I get to live in the freedom He provides through this gift.

On the days that I fully accept this as truth, I feel a huge weight lifted off me. I have the joy that comes along with this freedom.

I just have to be careful not to allow the lie to creep back into my mind. I continually remind myself of the way Dr. David Jeremiah explains this in *The Jeremiah Study Bible*:

> What it means for you: Freedom in Christ Alone. Jesus plus or minus anything does not equal faith; it is a formula. Formulas do not free anyone. Instead, they compel us to create wearying lists of do's and don'ts that confine us, rules that restrict us, and ultimately a false gospel that steals the joy of a relationship with the lover of our souls. Only faith in Christ alone leads to freedom. And that freedom produces live-giving spiritual fruit in our lives by which we can bless others.[4]

The gospel is good news, I remind myself. When Jesus cried, "It is finished!" on the cross, all my sins were forgiven. When I read that truth and then decide I must help Him out by adding or subtracting from His work, I'm saying, "Lord, You weren't enough."

Don't take from the gospel; don't add to it—I hear that in Bible study. Jesus is enough! Nothing more, nothing less. In Him alone is my salvation, my righteousness, my joy—both now and in eternity. What I read that morning comes back to me:

> Why would Christ need to die for our unrighteousness if we could earn our way back to God by our own efforts? That would make His coming unnecessary. To

---

4   David Jeremiah, *The Jeremiah Study Bible* (Franklin, Tennessee: Worthy Books, 2013), 1,625.

add human works to faith would be, as Paul said, to "set aside the grace of God." There is no need for grace if our good deeds could be sufficient for righteousness.[5]

A few minutes later, as I set the muffins on the table and talk to Billy about our day, I realize the second big lie that surfaces over and over is that God is busy and doesn't have time for my little problems. But I know this is not true. He gives every believer the gift of the Holy Spirit, and when we walk with Him in truth and obedience to His ways, the Holy Spirit (God's Spirit in us) gives us love, joy, peace, longsuffering, kindness, goodness, faithfulness, gentleness, and self-control (the fruit of the Spirit). These are the character traits that the Holy Spirit produces in a believer's life.

He is actively wanting and willing to walk me through my day if I will allow Him to do so.

As I sit down with the kids for a snack, I pick up a muffin. It's not perfect, as it didn't rise as much as I wanted, but it tastes divine. My life isn't perfect, but it's divinely influenced.

When I say my own prayers that night, I commit to walking with Him every day.

---

5   Ibid.

CHAPTER 34

The Art of Parenting

NANCY

By spring of 2013, our life has become pretty routine. Although things are busy every day, I feel grateful for our family. Like most families, we have our disagreements and misunderstandings, but even with those times, we all realize how much better we are now, together.

The weekdays are all school and activities, so we're very glad we have the weekend, and especially Sunday as our family day. However, this particular Sunday, as we sit in our new church (Jeff's church), the message being taught seems inaccurate. There's just something about it that isn't quite right.

I quickly jot down the verse on the screen so I can look it up when we get home. After making the decision not to return to our old church, we gladly made the shift to Jeff's church, but lately, I feel a strong need to double-check some of the teaching.

After we have lunch, I grab my Bible and head outside, where the kids are playing Marco Polo in the pool. I pray and ask God to show me, and then I look up the verse I jotted down during service. It's not the same as the verse in my Bible. I look up some commentary and find that the teaching from the church is not biblically accurate. Knowing I'm now hyperalert to this since my old church experience, I look at several more commentaries. It becomes clear that I need to discuss this with Jeff.

Why is it so difficult to just follow the Bible? Why do religions or churches claim to do so but then end up using it incorrectly?

That evening, Jeff and I talk it over, and we both decide we need to find a church that teaches word for word through the Bible. We're not interested in a church that uses Scripture out of context or, even worse, does not follow the Bible's instruction (like my old church). I feel so grateful to God for making it so clear to us. I realize that if I did not know the Bible, I would never have recognized the misrepresentation in that sermon. Even though it means we need to change churches, I am very grateful to know.

Weekday mornings are busy with getting everyone out the door, with three different schools in all different directions. It's not easy to get everyone where they need to be, but we manage.

Today, after everyone is gone, I straighten up the house, then grocery shop and run errands. Before I know it, it's time to do the afternoon school pickup, prepare snacks, and oversee homework.

I walk into the kitchen to start dinner. Since everyone will be home tonight, I want to make something special. I decide on nachos—although it's not a special meal to me, the kids are all very happy on nachos nights.

As I pour the chips onto the sheet pan, I hear Billy in the family room playing a commercial for a movie. I move to the end of the counter, where I can see him in front of the TV.

He typically goes through our recorded shows, usually cooking shows, and finds commercials for movies he wants to see. After it ends, he pauses the screen so the title of the movie remains, then he looks over at me. This is my cue to narrate for him.

"Oh, Billy, that looks like a good movie." I open the fridge and quickly grab a tomato and the hunk of cheese. "Let me come over and watch that commercial with you."

I sit with him on the couch, and he plays it again, being sure to pause it with the name on the screen. I stand up and walk over to the screen so I can point to the title as I read it.

"*Monsters University*," I read while pointing to the words.

Billy smiles and plays it again.

When he pauses again, I comment, "I think you would like to see this movie, *Monsters University*."

Since he has now heard me say it a couple of times, he says the title out loud. "*Monsters Anniversary*."

Since *university* is not a word he knows, he has substituted it with one he has heard before. He plays the commercial once again to be absolutely sure I understand that we will be seeing this movie.

I return to finish prepping the nachos before looking up the release date of the movie.

Oh, great. The release date is June 21.

This is a problem.

During the school year, we always wait until the movie has been out at least a month, and we go to the theater on a school day. This helps us avoid a crowded lobby and theater where the potential for Billy to be overloaded is almost certain. A summer release date means we cannot go to the theater.

The release date for the DVD will be in four to six months. That will work. This will be a movie we see in our living room.

The only downside, and it's a big one, is that we will be watching this commercial multiple times daily for about six months.

Once the nachos are in the oven, I go into Billy's room. I take his calendar, flip to November, and write the name of the movie on the box for Saturday November 23. If it comes out sooner, that is not a problem, but I like to give us a date far enough out so we are certain to watch it on or before that date.

Now the fun begins. Each morning, we look at the calendar and talk about how exciting it will be to watch the movie. When Billy plays the commercial and pauses it on the screen, we sit together, and I draw a picture of the screen or do the letters in block form so we can color it in. We count together to see how many days are left. I find out more about the characters so we can make a list to read together. We draw pictures and leave them in Colin's room. The next day, we draw pictures for Riley, followed by drawings for Jessica, then Colin again.

The plus side of this is that it gives us a built-in way to interact with Billy each day. We are so proud of Colin, Riley, and Jessica for watching this commercial every single day of their summer and acting just as excited as Billy is, but I am looking forward to the arrival of the DVD.

Finally on October 31, the DVD arrives.

Saturday, November 2, we all sit down on our sectional to watch the long-awaited *Monsters University*. It's a sweet movie, and we all enjoy it.

As I tuck Billy in for the night, I cannot help but laugh, because I know that first thing tomorrow morning, he will find a new movie. At least with the school year underway, the countdown will be a couple of months at most.

Life with Billy is both a blessing and a test of our patience. But he isn't our only concern.

Jeff and I settle into bed after a very long day. Before drifting off to sleep, we talk about the kids and how they are doing.

Of all the kids, Riley is the least of our concerns. She learned "life lessons" from the time she was born. I talked to her and taught her from such an early age that she often reminds me I'm repeating something she already knows. She's active in dance team, loves her school, and has a very good group of friends. As an added bonus, she loves spending time with Jeff and me.

Jessica is still quiet and less social. She's been struggling with some social anxiety, which is, of course, concerning. We're not sure exactly why, but she is also struggling to hold on to friends. Possibly she is just too shy, and that is getting in her way. She is super blessed to have Riley, who continues in the friend role they have long established and also does an amazing job as a big sister. Jeff and I are glad that since Jessica is younger, we know we have more time to teach her needed life lessons. For now, we just ease off and let her adjust to having such a large family. We are certain she will come around.

Tonight our focus is on Colin.

Colin has come a long way in the few years Jeff and I have been married. Since he was twelve years old when we married, we knew we only had a few years to help him learn more life skills and become responsible. Tonight we discuss how we are now seeing our hard work pay off. At first, it was an uphill battle, but now we are seeing it happen. He is responsible for getting himself up, making his own breakfast, and getting himself to the bus stop by 6:20 a.m.

Since his grandparents did everything for him during his early years, we are very glad he has now taken the initiative to learn and grow up.

For the time being, three out of four kids seem to be doing okay.

Why do we feel like we're waiting for a shoe to drop?

CHAPTER 35

Escalation

NANCY

Several weeks later, I note that something isn't right about Billy. He has suddenly developed a series of problems, including sensitivity to sunlight, sounds, and at times, even the sight of us. It's like he's uncomfortable in his own skin. He can't relax. He can't calm down. The slightest little thing sends him over the edge, and he starts yelling.

Our bedtime routine also changes. He cannot handle much. Brushing his teeth is a ten-second affair now—if I'm lucky. He falls into bed some nights just wanting to be left alone. Only a few days ago, we did butterfly kisses with our eyelashes and then Eskimo kisses with our noses, laughing. That's all gone now. He can barely stand the process of running up the stairs and using the bathroom. Some nights, he runs directly to his bedroom and flops into bed with his clothes on.

It seems like severe anxiety. But why? Everyone—moderators and moms in my autism Facebook group—says "autism and puberty." But why is it so extreme?

Thankfully, his immune specialist suggests that part of the problem causing anxiety is his school setting. We decrease his school day to two hours and change his classroom to a quiet one-on-one space with his teacher. The bus now also seems to cause him distress. He shakes in the morning while waiting for its arrival. Many days, I end up driving him, and eventually we cancel the bus, hoping to lessen his stress.

Since his school is a thirty-minute drive away, I stay in the area and grocery shop or read in the school lobby. Every day when I pick him up, he gets upset as I talk for a couple of minutes with his teacher. Even with the special accommodations, he continues to have what I think is severe anxiety.

In early 2014, his immune specialist suggests we take him out of school and begin a home tutoring program. We feel blessed the first day his tutor arrives. She was one of the aides in his classroom when he was five years old. He loves her, and they work well together for an hour each day.

We now focus on building his immune system through good nutrition. Thankfully, his doctor recommends a book that details the vitamins and minerals in the foods he eats. That helps me to be sure he is getting the nutrients he needs even with his limited diet. We focus on getting plenty of down time and good sleep, and we limit stress while still having him do some structured schoolwork.

We manage for several months, but it doesn't get any better.

Before leaving the house with Billy, I have to do due diligence to ensure that his surroundings will cause as little distress as possible. For example, today we head to the pediatrician for a checkup.

Because Billy has trouble with babies and toddlers—their crying can set off a full-blown panic attack—I call ahead to check the status of the waiting room and to be sure we can quickly make our way to an exam room if needed.

Once we're near the office, I circle the block several times so we won't arrive any earlier than our appointment time. I breathe a sigh of relief and thank God when we make it through the lobby and up the stairs into an empty waiting room.

But within minutes of signing in, Billy becomes stressed—he won't sit down or watch a movie.

My mind races. *What's happening? Why can't he remain calm?* The waiting room is empty. There is a Disney movie playing. Less than a year ago, he could sit with me in a full waiting room with thirty others, watching a Disney movie while kids cried and people chatted, and he was fine. *Why can't he handle an empty waiting room?*

I ask if we can go to a room. I am praying and hoping that will help. It doesn't.

Soon after the pediatrician enters, Billy is pacing and holding his head. Then he yells. I ask for ibuprofen for what is possibly a headache. It doesn't kick in quickly enough for him to calm down. The pediatrician is at a loss and ends up writing a referral for a neurologist.

Billy and I run for the van in the handicap parking at the front of the building. As I drive, he continues to yell and throw his toys all over. I'm a sobbing mess by the time we make it home. Billy enters the house and collapses into his chair, still yelling.

As soon as I can pull myself together, I call the neurologist. It's hard to describe the severity of the situation over the phone. When I'm offered the first available appointment in October and placed on a waiting list, I feel numb. Something is horribly wrong, and October is two months away.

Billy has always had his challenges, but somehow, I was able to help him. We are a team. He trusts me, and I have always found solutions to whatever distresses him. But now nothing I try works, and seeing him like this is more than I can take. Even if we can wait until October to see the neurologist, how will I safely get him there? I think back to all the things we did just a year ago. We had no problems going out for dinner. He recently had a birthday party at Pump It Up and raced through the tunnels with me. We even slid down the slide together. We went to Disneyland, and although we had accommodations like being able to avoid waiting in lines, he could do it. Billy and I even traveled to an immune specialist in Los Angeles. We stayed in a hotel for two nights so tests could be run.

Now, we can't even manage a fifteen-minute appointment within a couple of miles of our home.

I try turning to prayer, but it is hard. I feel so hopeless and distraught. I just keep asking God to heal Billy, and when that doesn't happen, it makes everything worse for me. When God does not do a miracle healing, I am absolutely devastated. I feel like I must not be praying correctly or like I must be doing something wrong.

Jeff and I jump online and search for another neurologist, and we are fortunate to find one who understands the severity of the situation and arranges a home visit the following week. She orders lab work and specialty tests. She prescribes a mood stabilizer. I've never been a fan of medications, but I'm desperate to help Billy, so I agree to try the mood stabilizer.

Unfortunately, the medication does not provide more than slight relief. It seems like everything causes him to become distressed. We are incredibly grateful when his episodes only last forty-five minutes, as some days there are many, and they consume most of the day. He just seems agitated by the littlest thing.

Jeff and I are distraught. Once an episode starts, I try everything to intervene. Nothing helps. We just have to wait. But the episodes end as quickly as they begin.

This pattern continues daily. We become grateful for the good days when Billy only has two hours total of extreme agitation or obsessive-compulsive disorder (OCD). I take notes on everything to see if I can figure out the triggers.

Nothing.

Nothing seems to trigger them, and nothing makes them better.

This situation with Billy is difficult for all of us. Colin doesn't say much—he's in high school and gone a lot, so that's helpful. We're homeschooling Jessica now, which has eased her anxiety. We're very glad that her room is on the other side of the house, so she rarely hears Billy, especially while wearing her earbuds to do her schoolwork.

Riley grew up with Billy and has never seen him like this before, so she's taking it hard. She has always been close to Billy, and since her toddler years, she has been able to help him, play with him, and just spend time with him. This is no longer the case.

When the yelling or repetitive noises become too much, she often escapes to our small shed in the backyard, which has a sofa and table in it. It also helps that she goes to her dance studio several afternoons a week. But like me, Riley has always been able to help Billy, and she is finding it heartbreaking.

Even more heartbreaking, I know she needs me to help comfort her, and I'm so heartbroken myself that I end up not being there for her. I am grateful that on Billy's good days, which now seem few and far between, I am able to slip out of the house to drive her to dance. That gives us a little time to talk and catch up.

CHAPTER 36

Anything but Typical

NANCY

It's 4:30 a.m., my typical wakeup time.

As quietly as possible, I leave my bed to head downstairs. I have to be strategic to avoid stepping on any of the spots that creak. Since it's so early and I have barely slept, I'm also careful not to miss a step or slip on the stairs.

I turn on the sunlamp. It's shocking how bright it is, but it's exactly the jolt I need to get in gear for what I know will be a tough day ahead.

My immediate goal, besides coffee, is to quietly make Billy's breakfast before he comes downstairs. He sometimes gets up as early as five, and if it's later than five thirty, I consider the extra time a big blessing. I know the odds of him not doing well are extremely high, and anything I can do to have things ready for him will help.

On the mornings when I have time between getting his food ready and hearing his door open, I sit on the sofa under the bright sun lamp and search my Bible for answers on healing. I write God's promises in my journal. I search for hope. I search for peace. Then I sit in the dark and pray.

I dread the sound of Billy's door opening. His OCD has increased dramatically, and some days it takes him an hour to walk downstairs. Each stair step requires multiple steps, in his mind. Touch toes to the edge, then lift the heel up in the air, come down flat-footed, then repeat. Each step takes several minutes, and sometimes he returns to the top of the stairs to start over, as if he thinks he did something wrong.

When I hear the door creak and then Billy's loud footsteps on the stairs, my stomach winds up in knots. I can only manage half a breath. Nothing in life is as difficult as seeing my child not doing well every day. The absence of his anxiety or OCD for an hour here and there becomes what I am most grateful for.

I watch as he comes downstairs and makes his way into the bathroom. On the days when he spends an hour or more getting downstairs, no one else can be on the stairs. On weekends, it's not a problem, but on school days, we all need access. Once he makes it to the bathroom, gets changed, and comes to the family room, we can begin our day, but I never know what will happen.

I hold my breath as I peek into the family room to see him. At best, he is able to tolerate seeing or hearing me, but some days he becomes very irritated by the sight of me in his space.

Most mornings, after he frantically takes his medications and eats his food too fast, I slip out of the room and pray that he can calm down.

More often than not, I hear him make noises that indicate he is about to lose it. When he loses it, he dumps his entire bin of toys onto the tile floor. I sob as I listen to him struggle, partly because he isn't doing well, and partly because if anyone is still trying to sleep, that becomes nearly impossible.

The struggle is internal for him, so I do not know the cause or the solution. When he does recover, I quietly enter the room to see him picking up his toys and returning them to his toy bin. He is such a sweet boy. Tears run down my face as I watch him clean up the mess he made, knowing he did not *want* to do this at all.

Whenever Billy is yelling, I pray, but it's hard because I feel so hopeless. I know I've fallen back into my old way of thinking—that God gave this to me to solve, but I can't seem to pull myself out of that old thinking. Because of my religious background, I only pray for a big healing for Billy. When God does not do a miracle healing, I am absolutely devastated.

I start thinking once again that I must be doing something wrong since God isn't helping us.

Even though Jeff and I are really struggling with everything going on with Billy, we remain determined to give our other three kids as much of a normal life as possible. With Jessica's thirteenth birthday right around the corner, Riley and I begin a secret project. We decide to redecorate Jessica's room as a surprise gift. Several Saturdays in a row, we spend the afternoon shopping for new bedding, pillows, and wall decor. We settle on the colors turquoise and white so the decor will match her walls.

On her birthday, Jeff takes her out early in the morning for breakfast and then to visit her grandparents. Riley and I enlist Colin's help moving her bed and shifting a bookcase to a different wall. By two p.m., the room is all set up. When Jessica returns home, she is all smiles.

In addition to celebrating her birthday, I also have good news about a volunteer position she is interested in. Since homeschooling limits her social interaction, I have been searching for another option for her to be out of the house. She has her classes at the homeschool co-op, but that is only one day a week, so the volunteer position at the preschool she herself attended is great news to her. She had to wait until she was thirteen before they would allow her to volunteer, and that day has finally arrived.

Most days, Riley is out the door early for school, then after school she has dance team practice or texts me asking if she can go home with a friend. She's in high school, so her social calendar is pretty full. She also has many dance workshops, weekend camps, and even weeklong dance camps or performances during school breaks. Although we miss spending as much time with her as we used to, we are also so blessed that she is able to be away from the house to avoid some of Billy's tough times. Sleepovers at friends' homes become a regular weekend activity for Riley, and while I'm happy for her, I miss the days when Billy was better and we could host the sleepovers.

On the rare weekends when she's home, Jeff and I really enjoy having dinner with her and watching a favorite show, like *Gilmore Girls*—which Jeff constantly forgets the name of and ends up calling *Girls of Gilmore*. Of course, there are not too many dads who would watch *Girls of Gilmore* with their wife and teenage daughter.

CHAPTER 37

Patience

JEFF

I back out of the driveway on my way to the grocery store to pick up bananas, bok choy, eggs, and whatever else Nancy has added to the list. She often texts me while I'm shopping to let me know what else we need. If the text comes in after I have completed the shopping, I turn right back around and return to the store.

That might seem over the top to most people, but it's the least I can do for my wife.

Of course, today she may not text. It's been a rough morning. For some reason, Billy did not sleep, and Nancy was up most of the night with him. Again. Which means that, even though she tells me to sleep, that there's no need for both of us to suffer, my rest is sporadic at best.

It's been like this for days now—so many, I've actually lost count. The doctors have made suggestions, but the only thing we've found that works is to wait for the string of sleepless nights to run its course.

On days like this, I should have more patience, more grace, and more compassion. Instead, I am short-tempered. All I want is for things to be better. Better for Billy. Better for Nancy. Better for all of us. And in my frustration, I end up taking it out on Nancy at a time when she is at her breaking point.

In all fairness, she's sleep deprived. It doesn't take much to set her off. Last night, she spent the whole night drinking coffee while waiting for the sun to come up. Now the entire day will be spent just trying to get through it, and like Nancy says, "For what? To do it all again tonight?"

I listen to her frustration. I try not to say anything stupid, but then I do it.

Before I filter through the implications of my words, I blurt out, "It's going to get better."

Ooh boy. This really sets her off.

Do I *know* it's going to get better? No, I don't. I *want* it to get better for all our sakes, but do I know it will? Nope.

That was the point in the conversation when I knew it was best for me to give her some space, so I offered to run to the store.

Now I stroll through the store, waiting for her text but also trying to regroup. As I push the cart mindlessly up and down each aisle, I silently pray. *God, You know our situation. You see what this is doing to us. You see what this is doing to my wife. Please, God, help us. We need help. I need help so I don't make a bad situation even worse. I know You hear me, but I need You to help me.*

After about twenty minutes of this, I decide the text isn't forthcoming. Maybe Nancy has managed to nod off. Best not to send a "just-checking" text that might *ping* her awake and achieve the opposite of its intended purpose.

I check out and take my small bag of essentials to the car. As I maneuver out of the parking lot and head toward home, I hear my phone *ping* with that incoming text I'd given up on earlier. I pull over to read:

> *I am so sorry. I'm sorry for yelling at you. Please forgive me.*

That makes me smile. I continue reading:

> *If you are still there, please get coconut milk, a few apples, and some of that cheesy popcorn. When you get home, can we eat popcorn, drink root beer, and watch something stupid on TV?*

I happily turn the car around and return to the store, knowing the checkout clerk is going to laugh. She knows that the first time I go through the checkout is usually not the last time she will see me that day.

Once I've reparked, I send Nancy a quick text before going back into the store:

I'm sorry too. Of course I forgive you. I'm sorry everything is so hard. I will be home soon, and I would love to watch stupid TV with you.

Twenty minutes later, I pull into our garage, enter the house, and note with relief that Billy is silent and calm. I walk upstairs to find Nancy waiting with root beer and bowls for our cheesy popcorn. I hug her and tell her again, "I forgive you."

Thank You, God, for helping us get through. Things are really hard, but I know You know the reasons.

CHAPTER 38

Surrender

NANCY

Although life has been difficult for Billy for the whole past year, our feeling of helplessness finally brings us to our knees.

With meltdowns that come out of nowhere and can be long-lasting, Jeff and I are overwhelmed. We never know what each day will bring, and that keeps us on edge. Either we're praying that God will prevent the next episode, or we're praying and yelling at God to stop them. Each night we climb into bed exhausted, knowing that the next day will likely bring more of the same.

I am grateful to my prayer warrior friends. I can text Gia, Sherry, Brooke, and Kellie anytime, and they will pray. Knowing that friends are praying for relief is so comforting.

Billy's neurologist runs additional lab work and prescribes another medication, yet the episodes continue every day. Everything we do to prevent his meltdowns—eliminating all noise in the house, limiting movement around him, spending hours researching and searching for answers through exhaustion and tears—does nothing.

We are devastated that this is happening to Billy, but we are just as devastated that our three other kids have to live like this. They cannot make a sound. If someone is going to sneeze, they have to run to the other side of the house. Need to cough? Don't do it anywhere near Billy. Want to have friends over? Sure, you can do that. But only in the backyard. This is no way for them to live.

But we're truly amazed at how well they handle it. I'm not sure I could have handled any of this at their age, but they do it and all without complaint. Every night, as I pray, I say to God, "Thank You. And please, Lord, bless Colin, Riley, and Jessica for handling this."

Finally his neurologist orders a specialty test, and Billy is diagnosed as having something called PANDAS—pediatric autoimmune neuropsychiatric disorders associated with streptococcal infections. PANDAS affects motor skills, concentration, coordination, and sensitivity to light and sound—all things we've noted with Billy. Plus, it produces OCD and tics, and Billy has developed both.

But even with this diagnosis, not much of what his neurologist suggests seems to help. Every day is the same, with no end in sight. I barely leave the house, and if I do, I return as quickly as possible. I can't stand to see Billy struggling so much, yet I have to be home when he is. I am at my breaking point.

During this painful time, I order and read every Christian book I can find on healing, how and why God answers prayers, and how to pray. I want to find the right formula so God will heal Billy. I read . . . I pray . . . I cry . . . I yell. I memorize Scripture. I yell at God about not holding up His end of the bargain. He healed all the people in the books I read. Why not Billy?

Months later, we finally get Billy in to see a PANDAS specialist, who starts homeopathy treatments. In short order, Billy becomes more like his old self, watching DVDs and bouncing on his trampoline while playing with his musical instruments—all a long way from sitting in his chair and holding his head or throwing his toys in anger.

This starts to feel like our long-awaited answer to prayer. The more I learn about homeopathy remedies, the more I realize that they can bring about healing. They help in the moment, but the right remedy also causes the body to begin a healing process.

But even with the homeopathy treatment, I have to stay alert. I take notes daily so we can determine when he will need a dose. His doctor realizes, early on in her treatment, that Billy is very sensitive, and if given too often, the homeopathy remedy itself can cause aggravation. Although some of her patients do take their remedy daily, Billy is someone who takes it as needed. If I can see signs that he isn't doing well before it's a full-blown meltdown, I can get the remedy in him. But, once it starts, there is no possibility. It is a real balancing act, but when I get it right, it leads to much better days.

Thank God.

One particular morning, the sound of a Thomas the Tank Engine song accompanied by Billy's tambourine jingle gives me a sense of unbelievable relief. From that point forward, whenever I hear that song in the morning, I smile. It signals the start to a good day. It's funny how my definition of a good day has changed.

It's simple. A good day is any day that Billy is enjoying himself. That is all I need. The trees out the window look greener. I hear the birds and watch them out the kitchen window. I feel grateful. Grateful to see Billy up and moving. Seeing him happy is something I will never take for granted. Although he still has his rough days, the fact that he isn't as reactive to noise, hyperalert to the sight of us, or stuck in OCD behavior gives me incredible joy.

But as Billy's sensitivity to noise is still an issue due to PANDAS, we have to figure out ways to keep sounds to a minimum. The base of the blender finds its new home on the garage workbench. In fact, although the screwdrivers and wrenches still hang on the pegboard, the entire counter space is devoted to our mini garage kitchen. We now have a freezer, refrigerator, toaster oven, and microwave in the garage. This allows Colin, Riley, and Jessica to get snacks when they want without upsetting Billy.

Some days we joke about having the best-smelling garage in town.

We also classify a day as either a Crock-Pot day or a pressure cooker day. If the morning goes well, I put together a meal for the Crock-Pot. That way if things go south in the afternoon, we will still have a meal. If the morning is rough, we have the pressure cooker for a quick meal in the evening.

Seeing my child struggling this much is the worst emotional pain I've ever felt. I cannot breathe. I can't focus on anything else, and really, nothing else matters. All my to-do lists just sit. The dust and piles of stuff around the house continue to grow—I don't care. I only have two goals: help Billy and give our other kids the best life we can. I enjoy the moments when Billy is able to interact some. I sit with him, hugging him. I thank God for him. When he is in an OCD loop and unable to break free of it, I can barely hold it together.

I eventually set out on a quest to find the answer to my big question: *Why, God? Why do You answer my prayers sometimes, and other times I feel like You don't hear or, even worse, that You don't care?* I want to know why, of course, but I also know that God does not always tell us why. It really isn't His job to keep me informed. I mean, He is God, after all.

I go into my bathroom and sit on the floor sobbing. I pound my fists on the floor and yell at God. I tell Him He doesn't care. Then I say, "You have no idea what it is like to see your child in pain."

In that next moment, I feel a peaceful reminder that I'm wrong about that.

It is this realization that God understands my situation better than any parent ever could that propels me to surrender Billy to Him. I replace my negative thoughts with truth from Scripture.

I also pray for strength to endure and to accept and not question His plan.

CHAPTER 39

Road Trip 2015: "Life Is a Highway"

NANCY

Each year since we married, our kids have looked forward to our family road trip. Since we aren't a typical family—one in which all the kids are able to tell you what they think or want—the trip isn't about what we see and do once we reach our vacation spot. It is about our time together in a comfortable rental home with the best view we can afford. The kitchen has to be well supplied, as we cook all our meals. At this point, if Billy is able to venture out, it will be for just an hour here and there, and most of our time will be spent indoors playing board games.

Our plan this year, which we think is workable, is to rent a house within two hours or so of our home. This means we can drive straight there without any bathroom breaks. We have not had any successful outings for over a year without substantial planning. A bathroom break in an unknown area could prove to be more than Billy can manage.

Riley creates a social story for Billy, in which she works in a new toy I ordered for him—Benny the Bull. Billy is going to Benny's house! I figure since Benny the Bull is a toy Billy requested, he may be willing to get in the car to go to Benny's house. Riley takes pictures of the vacation house and adds Benny the Bull to them.

Everything is in order. As I prepare food and complete the packing, Jeff is busy getting the van ready. Our plan is to leave our house about two p.m. for our four o'clock check-in.

At around one in the afternoon, I hear the sounds of a meltdown. I hold my breath as I tiptoe toward the kitchen to peek around the corner. It's starting—Billy is stuck in a loop; I can see him flipping through his DVDs, trying to make a choice but then closing the folder that holds them only to open it again and try to choose one. He shouts.

I move back around the corner, and I hear his toys flying, hitting the tile floor, with some sliding under the couch. Our plans are about to change.

Everything is very tricky with Billy. If I had known this was coming on, I could have given him the homeopathic to prevent it. Once the episode is underway, getting Billy to cooperate with taking anything is nearly impossible. It's very difficult to figure out when and how often to resort to the remedy. He can seem absolutely fine one minute and then just crumble into a big mess the next.

Shaking, I head upstairs and sit on my bed as the tears carve a path down my cheeks. I'm at a complete loss as to what to do. Once Billy is at this level, I'm unable to reach him.

I'm numb. Jeff comes upstairs to comfort me, and I sob as I recite out loud the Scriptures I know—God's promises for good.

I yell at God. "Really? This is the plan You have for us? We don't ask for much, and now we cannot even take an annual family trip? I don't understand . . . I don't understand . . . I don't understand . . ."

Once I've managed to calm down, Jeff and I discuss solutions.

"So . . ." He holds up his index finger like he's counting. "You can stay home with Billy while I take the other kids on our family trip. Then you and Billy can try to join us tomorrow."

I close my eyes, struggling to get over my disappointment. The drive together as a family is one of the best parts of the trip. We listen to our playlist of songs, eat our snacks, and play Mad Libs. I cannot stand the thought of missing all of this.

He continues, counting on a second finger. "Or we wait till Billy recovers, and we all travel today in two separate cars, just in case you have to turn around and bring Billy home."

I frown. That doesn't seem like a good option either.

We cannot come up with a solution that will allow our family to be together for something so important. It breaks my heart that with everything our children have endured in the past year, we cannot at least keep this tradition.

I close my eyes and begin to pray . . . *really* pray in a way I haven't before, with complete reliance on Him.

Within fifteen minutes, Billy has recovered.

God has faithfully answered, and although I am still holding my breath, our family climbs into the van.

In spite of what now feels like nothing more than a minor setback, we're on our way.

Every year, we have chosen a theme song for our vacation. During the drive there and back home, we play the songs in order on our trips. I'm just about to play the first song, when Billy starts playing "Life Is a Highway," by Rascal Flatts, on his iPod. It seems to me that Billy has chosen this song from his favorite movie, *Cars*, as a way to cope with being in the van with his entire family.

Instead of our usual playlist, our other kids—who by now really understand Billy's coping methods—pop in their earbuds and listen to their own music while attempting to drown out "Life Is a Highway," which Billy plays over and over and over again.

Two and a half hours later, as we pull into the driveway of our vacation rental house, we are still listening to "Life Is a Highway." It is mind-numbing, but we are just grateful we made the trip.

Once inside, I set Benny the Bull on the sofa, and Billy scoops the toy right up.

Then he says, "Home!"

I look at Jeff, a sense of helplessness overwhelming me. Although I'm able to calm him some, he continues to quietly repeat, "Home."

Our five-day trip turns into three, and we head home—once again listening to "Life Is a Highway" for the entire drive.

Life is indeed a highway, with more unplanned detours than I care to count.

When August rolls around, it's time to get all the paperwork for school done. We still have three different schools to deal with, so it's a lot.

We want to be sure we get all the checks written for everyone's extracurriculars. Riley is on the dance team, so the calendar fills up quickly with her after-school practices, camps, competitions, and football halftime performances.

Since Colin is in band and playing rugby, his schedule is pretty full too. We are relieved when we have it all on a calendar and see that the big events are on different days.

One of our challenges with Jessica being homeschooled is a lack of extracurricular activities. With her heart condition, we also have limitations as far as what kind of activities she can do.

We are very fortunate to have a homeschool co-op near our house. They have a lot of activities and classes, and when Jessica hears about a guitar class, she is all in! They meet once a week and learn songs, and they'll even have an end-of-the-year performance. Perfect!

Jeff and I are grateful beyond belief that Riley, Colin, and Jessica have had a fun summer and are looking forward to a good school year. Three out of four seems pretty good.

CHAPTER 40

Ups and Downs

NANCY

In spite of Billy's improvement when the homeopathics can be administered in time, he's still suffering. I explain to his doctor that he seems to get stuck in an OCD loop, especially when he is trying to watch a movie or a TV show. It's a favorite activity, and he has the entire room to himself, so I'm not sure at all what is causing his distress. I also share with her how sad I am that he can no longer attend his therapeutic horseback riding program or music therapy—both activities he loved.

This particular morning, I have done all I can. Billy's food is on the table under where the TV is mounted on the wall. I pray he'll come out of the bathroom, get his food, and sit down to eat.

I instead watch helplessly as he comes out of the bathroom and heads straight for the DVD player. He opens and closes it, bobbing his head up and down. He follows that action with five steps of his right leg to the side, then five steps back to the center. Over and over, I watch as his OCD and tics take control. Over and over, the same pattern. He is stuck. Bend over the DVD player, open and close, bob of the head. Five steps out, five steps back in, open and close the DVD player.

After ten minutes, I feel like I might lose my mind.

What are we missing? We know the cause, PANDAS, so why can't we find the cure? Better yet, why won't God cure him? I don't understand, and it's breaking my heart. There isn't anything I wouldn't do, say, or spend. God, please just tell me, and I'll do it!

I watch as he finally sits down to eat, and I breathe a sigh of relief that at least he will get food in his body. But five seconds later, he is back up, and the process starts again. Open, close, bob, stomp. *How do we live like this? Why do we have to? Why can't I help him?*

We do know that PANDAS is brought on by strep bacteria. We have treated the strep infection, but the effect on Billy's brain lingers.

I can't watch. His brain is short-circuiting and causing all this strange repetitive behavior, and he can't stop.

I finally hear the DVD start, and he sits on the couch and begins to eat. One minute later, he is back up. Open, close, bob, stomp. Open, close, bob, stomp . . .

As I'm watching him, my cell phone vibrates. Even though it's a number I don't recognize, I escape to the garage to answer.

"Hello." It's an unfamiliar woman's voice. "Is William available?"

William? Does she mean Billy?

"I'm his mom. Can I help you?"

"This is Veronica with Health First Insurance. Is this William's number?"

Now she has my attention. I've been waiting for them to call. Our old insurance company has made changes in coverage that have necessitated our changing companies. "He goes by Billy, and he has autism, so I'm the one you need to—"

"I actually need to speak directly with William . . . I mean Billy." Her manner is off-putting. "Is there a better number for him?"

"Billy is not capable of conversation. He has low-functioning autism. I'm the one who can—"

"Billy is eighteen, correct?"

"Yes, he is, but he is not capable of talking with you. We are in the process of getting his conservatorship done." This is true. On top of everything else, we'd been going through the red tape involved in the process of becoming Billy's official legal conservators.

"Well, in that case, I can speak with you," the woman concedes.

"Oh, good." I breathe a sigh of relief.

"I just need his permission."

Feeling a little feisty, I question if this woman has heard a word I've said. But I really don't want to waste my precious energy by arguing. I force a smile. "Let me see what I can do."

I walk back into the family room, where Billy is sitting on the couch. Thankfully, he is calm at the moment, so I sit down beside him. I put the phone on speaker and hold it in front of him.

"Okay," I say in to the phone. "He's listening."

"Hi, Billy." The woman's slightly condescending tone hasn't shifted one bit. "This is Veronica with Health First. I'm wondering if I can get your permission to speak with your mother?"

At this point, Billy begins squealing at Thomas the Tank Engine rounding the bend of the track. He jumps up in front of the TV. I follow him with the phone in hand. I hold it in front of him, being sure to hold on tight so he doesn't knock it out of my hand as he jumps up and down while watching the scene.

When he finally stops squealing, I whisper to him, "Billy, say yes." Silence.

"Billy . . ." A little louder. "Say yes."

Without taking his eyes off the TV, Billy says, "Billy, say yes" in a loud whisper—obviously just wanting me to leave him alone.

"Veronica," I whisper into the phone. "Did you hear him?"

"Yes." She clears her throat. "Yes, I did."

I try hard not to burst out laughing as I return to the garage to have the needed conversation.

A few days after the Veronica-the-insurance-lady incident, Billy and I are headed from an appointment with Dr. Thomas, Billy's bio cranial doctor, and then directly to speech with Miss Karrie. Billy loves speech therapy, so I'm feeling less stressed than usual.

Over a year has passed since Billy's difficulties started in 2014. We leave little to chance. If we have an upcoming appointment somewhere new to us, either Jeff or I visit the office to see where to park, where to enter, where a side or back entrance is located. How likely will we be to encounter a dog, a baby or toddler, or another person with special needs? Billy's reaction to anyone with unpredictable behavior sends him running to the van, yelling at the top of his lungs. It only takes a couple of experiences like this to know that when he runs, I can't keep up.

Despite our best planning, sometimes we miscalculate. Even so, we're sometimes delighted by Billy's response to something going haywire.

This particular day, knowing that I have to stretch a fifteen-minute drive to thirty minutes, I give Billy his snack and take a couple of detours. I circle around the roads near the office to be sure we don't arrive even a minute early. Waiting is not a concept Billy understands.

But suddenly, an unanticipated obstacle appears. Orange cones and large work trucks block the entrance to the parking lot. Not only will we be unable to park right next to the building's side entrance, we will not even be able to enter the parking lot.

In the past, this would have sent my heart racing, knowing that Billy's reaction and panic were about to set in. But today is different. Since we've seen God's healing hand in Billy's life over the past few months—thanks to the homeopathic treatments—I have a sense of calm.

I pull into the bank parking lot next door to the building we are heading to. Since the lot is fenced in, we will have to head back in the other direction and around the fence to walk the length of the parking lot. It feels like a miracle when Billy walks with me. He is calm. He is happy. He isn't fazed by the change in routine. I explain it to him anyway, but he gets it.

I can't wait to tell Jeff and the kids and anyone else who will listen. I'm so grateful. As I walk with him to the side entrance, I smile, as if it's the best day of my life. In some ways, it is. I keep saying to myself, *Thank You, God . . . Thank You.* Tears well up at the thought that we may be able to do more. Billy may be able to go places. The thought overwhelms me.

When we leave speech therapy fifty minutes later, I feel so proud of this boy who has worked so hard to overcome so much. Just a year ago, we barely left the house. His meltdowns consumed us. When he didn't have an OCD meltdown, it was a really good day. On the severe days, we were just grateful when the episode ended and he could have a few hours free of anxiety and OCD.

But now we have more frequent days like today. He isn't just free of pain; he is full of joy. He is walking the entire length of the parking lot without hurry or stress.

Thank You, God.

One day at a time.

CHAPTER 41

Learning to Rely on His Word

NANCY

Thanks to an assessment we have done of our home electrical system, we figure out that the smart meter (which reads our gas and electric usage) on the wall just outside Billy's bedroom is interfering with his ability to sleep. This, of course, leads to all kinds of daytime problems.

He is being "zapped" by both the Wi-Fi and the electricity. As he became increasingly ill, he also became more sensitive, and that resulted in his getting completely stuck in OCD patterns, especially in rooms where more electricity is in use. If he's near a Wi-Fi router, it's even worse.

It turns out that Billy is super-sensitive to EMF (Wi-Fi) and electricity. He can most likely feel it jolting his system, which is why he gets stuck in a loop of OCD behavior. I find a book titled *Zapped*, and it explains exactly what we are seeing with Billy.

Once we figure this out, we have an electrician install a type of switch where we can shut off electricity to portions of the house. We also change our Wi-Fi to be just powerful enough to support our stuff without being so powerful that it causes problems for Billy.

The other thing that helps is taking away all internet devices that Billy uses. He now has CDs, DVDs, a portable DVD player, and other non-internet toys. Although this helps alleviate about 50 percent of his meltdowns, they are still happening, but we are certainly grateful it's not as many times a day.

Full-time caregiving consumes most of our day and energy, but we have learned to simplify.

Colin is now in his first year of college and enjoying dorm life. As long as we can make life okay for Riley and Jessica, there are only five things on our to-do list each day. I consider the day successful if they all get done. This list includes:

1. Changing Billy's bed and washing the sheets.
2. Making meals.
3. Grinding coffee for the next day.
4. Loading the dishwasher after dinner.
5. Setting everything up for Billy for the next day.

All else must be flexible, changeable, and overlooked as needed. We certainly remember the easier days when everyone went to school and we had free time, but those days are long gone.

Jeff and I struggle with our exhausting life circumstances. Even though we've seen some improvements, we struggle with not knowing when or even if Billy will get well. We struggle with understanding that God hears our prayers and loves us when circumstances remain pretty much the same.

We have prayed for years now for God to heal Billy, and if I were to simply trust my circumstances or feelings, I would have to conclude that He doesn't hear me or doesn't love me or maybe doesn't even care.

However, I know that in the past God has heard me and has answered my prayers, and many times I have had to move forward step by step in faith that He would work it all out. And He has! Many times.

I remember what a miracle it was that Keith's first seizure occurred directly in front of the homes of a paramedic and a doctor. I look back at how He directed my path in leaving Keith and in providing complete clarity on where the kids and I would live, the schools they would attend, and a church where I would make friends.

God also answered Jeff and me when we prayed about getting married.

But after years of praying and not seeing consistent results with Billy, it's hard. Really hard. I have to rely on His Word and promises from the Bible. His promises are that He will be with me, guide me, and provide peace as I rely on Him. Although there are plenty of times when He has healed people, that is not one of His promises. So I have to accept that although He may choose to heal Billy, it is not a promise.

When I wake up during the night with a pain in the pit in my stomach, I have to recite verses to reassure myself of His love and care.

One night from two a.m. until nearly five, I whisper to myself, "You restore my soul You restore my soul" (Psalm 23:3). I say it over and over again to keep my thoughts from spinning out of control and to allow God to restore my soul in that moment. Otherwise, during the three hours I am awake, I would have spun myself in circles again trying to solve Billy's health problems.

I just need to trust and let God lead the way.

And He does. We are so blessed that we can dedicate some time to our other kids. We never want them to feel like they don't matter to us. Yes, we have a lot with Billy and his care, but any chance we have to spend time alone with our other three is a blessing.

We are able to carve out time to have lunch with Colin, either in between his college classes or on the weekends. Jessica gets built-in one-on-one time, thanks to the homeschooling.

Even though it is tricky, and often very touch-and-go until the last possible moment, both Jeff and I are able to attend Riley's Friday-night halftime dance performances. With the help of some good respite care or, even better, from my amazing friend Gia, we do not miss a single at-home game performance.

Usually, Jeff goes early to drop Riley off and then volunteers at the concession stand or as a ticket taker. I leave the house when he texts me the approximate time of her halftime performance. We sit together to watch her and cheer for fifteen minutes, then I head straight home while Jeff waits to bring Riley home after the game.

I cannot believe how far Billy has come in the last year, thanks to the homeopathic treatment and the Wi-Fi adjustment, and now I can't believe his latest setback. It hit within a week of his having dental work done. We believe the dental work stirred up the infection again that had caused strep symptoms and is now a lingering inflammation. Even with antibiotics, a new homeopathic remedy, and supplements, we can only wait for his body to fight it.

Since November, his OCD, anxiety, and inability to leave the house have impacted our entire day once again.

Since there have been multiple times when Billy has gotten up during the night, we have a doorbell on his door that chimes loudly in our bedroom. Most mornings, I'm awake prior to the *bing-bong*, as I prefer to not be startled by the sound.

Like every morning, I tiptoe into the kitchen to pack lunch for Riley and make breakfast. If I have prepared well the night before, it's just a matter of grabbing a couple of things from the fridge. On the mornings when I haven't prepared and I have to open the refrigerator or pick up a fork from the drawer, those slight noises will cause Billy distress.

Once Riley and Jeff are out the door, Billy's morning, like all mornings now, is spent carefully designing rows of his Little People. Today he spends hours and hours designing and redesigning them. The amount of time he devotes to having them each stand up is remarkable. He shows incredible determination and patience as they fall and he stands them back up. Apparently, since we removed the TV and DVD player due to his Wi-Fi and electricity sensitivity, this is his new OCD coping behavior.

If I attempt to interrupt or speed it up, he becomes upset. I do my best to stay out of the kitchen until he is done, but the days when his morning routine extends well into the afternoon can be difficult. I sit in the next room watching and waiting. Sometimes it seems as if he's close to being done with the morning setup, only to then knock it down and redo the entire arrangement.

It's hard to believe that just this past October, this morning process was completed in thirty to forty-five minutes. Now it takes up the first half of his day and sometimes as late as four in the afternoon. I can only comment when he finishes his masterpiece, which today happens at two.

Relieved, I rise and enter the kitchen. "Billy, you did a great job with those today. They're all standing up so perfectly. And it looks like Elmo and SpongeBob are friends. Good work."

Billy smiles, and he even lets out a laugh.

I'm so glad to see his sense of humor shine through. This means that although he clearly has had a setback, it's nowhere near as severe as they were a couple years ago.

CHAPTER 42

Day or Night

JEFF

It's the middle of the night when I wake up to the sound of Nancy down in the kitchen, obviously preparing food for Billy. I look at the clock. One a.m. I try to remember. *Did she even come to bed?*

When she comes back into the room to retrieve his water cup, I gruff out, "Have you been up all night?"

"No." She rubs her neck. "He just got up. But his bed needs to be changed, and he's hungry."

I get up to help change his sheets while Nancy finishes getting his food ready. Billy is full of energy—the kind of energy you would expect during the day, but not in the middle of the night. It's endearing in a way, but also very annoying.

Once he is fed and changed, I climb into his bed with him to help him settle down. He's happy to have me there, but he's very much wide awake. After about twenty minutes of trying to calm him, I realize how pointless it is. I return to our room to give Nancy the bad news. Although Billy will most likely stay in his room, it is doubtful he will be quiet enough for Nancy to sleep.

I get back into our bed and try to drift off, feeling very sad about our situation. This is the third night in a row, and although Nancy can usually handle two nights, by the third night, it really begins to take its toll.

At 5 a.m., while we sip our coffee and try to wake up, we hold hands and pray for our day. We have no idea how Billy will be. We pray for him to be calm and happy and just able to get through the day without too many meltdowns.

By midmorning, he's had a bath and breakfast and is settled in his room with his books. I look at Nancy and suggest she at least try to take a nap while he is quiet. She agrees, and as I head downstairs, I pray to God to give her some peaceful time to rest.

I look around at the pile of laundry from Billy's bed. The kitchen is a mess also. The middle-of-the-night meal preparation left some chaos in its wake. I look at the stack of mail and think I should probably go through it. Then I realize how completely exhausted I am. My exhaustion is not from lack of sleep; it's just exhaustion from this unpredictable and taxing life we have.

I grab a black cherry soda and a bag of chips, then head to the shelves that hold our DVD collection. I pop one into the player, then settle on the couch. On days like today, the goal is just to get through it. I will be ready to help Nancy later, but for now, all I can manage to do is sit and watch one of the movies that comfort me. I have seen it more times than I can count, but it gives me a break.

The good Lord knows, my brain needs a break.

CHAPTER 43

No Reason

NANCY

This morning it occurs to me that I have no reason for hope, at least not the way we are currently living.

I'm driving home from dropping Riley off at school. That's become our routine, and I love the morning drives with her. They are a little dose of sunshine for me. In fact, this morning before leaving the house, I called her "sunshine." On the half-hour drive to school, we talk, we laugh, we have the freedom to chat uninterrupted, which we can never do at home.

Our homelife used to involve having friends and family over. But now it's become entirely focused on not making any noise while we get ready to leave the house.

On the return drive today, I listen to music and pray and consider our daily circumstances. And though I have no reason to hope, I'm not depressed—and that is exactly my point. There's no *reason* for it, yet I have tremendous hope. It's a gift from God. I recognize it clear as day.

It isn't because of circumstances, because our circumstances stink. It isn't because I'm trying to have hope or pretending to have hope. It isn't me smiling through the pain. On many levels, I'm actually sad. I'm sad that Billy continues to be sick. I'm sad that God hasn't healed him (yet). I'm really sad that in spite of all my research and all the many doctors, nothing has provided more than a few steps forward only to be followed by a severe backslide. I'm sad that my other kids have to live the way they do. They have to know exactly where the floors creak and never step on those spots. They have to navigate their way around the house, always knowing where Billy is and his current ability to handle even seeing another person. They have to understand that although things may be stable for a moment, it can all change the next second.

The last three days have been especially hard, as we've been dealing with an unexpected concern: Billy, for the first time, started to serve himself food. He gets food out of the cupboards and fridge and dishes up his own meals.

Later that day, I walk into the kitchen very quietly. Billy is busy "reading" books while sitting on the couch—Billy doesn't so much *read* as commit certain words to memory. We were hopeful that the years of vision therapy and other therapies would help him with reading, but that has not been the case. My plan is to put the barbeque chicken leftovers in the Crock-Pot. If I set it on low for a couple of hours, they should be all ready for dinner. I can just dump a bag of salad mix in a bowl, and we should be good to go.

I look in the fridge, but the container of chicken is not where I left it. While closing the refrigerator door, I notice the empty container with a bit of barbeque sauce left in it, sitting open on the counter.

I run upstairs and try to catch my breath. "Jeff, Jeff. Did you take the chicken out of the fridge?"

"No." He smiles a little, no doubt at my rushed entrance, followed by a question about chicken. "Why?"

"It's gone. I was going to throw it in the Crock-Pot for dinner tonight, but it's all gone."

"How could it be gone?"

"That's the thing. The empty container is on the counter. I think Billy must have eaten it."

His eyebrows shoot up. "Oh my gosh. Billy ate our dinner?"

I nod. "All six chicken breasts."

Jeff and I rush downstairs and silently begin to remove food from the fridge. Since Billy does not understand portion control or his food allergies, we have to quickly move the food from the kitchen fridge to the garage fridge, and we have to do all this without Billy hearing us. Fortunately, he is into his books at the moment, so we move as fast as possible.

When Billy takes a bathroom break, we enlist Jessica's help. The three of us quickly fill laundry baskets with anything we can find containing gluten, dairy, sugar, or frankly anything processed, and run to the garage. I throw bags of cookies and boxes of crackers under blankets in the living room, making a mental note to return for them later before someone sits in the wrong place and pulverizes them.

The most dangerous foods go first, in hopes that the remaining food won't be touched until we can make another run.

Fortunately, we have a full-size freezer and refrigerator in the garage. It takes some serious reorganization to be sure the only foods in the kitchen refrigerator are safe for Billy to eat and are in the appropriate portions.

Trying to estimate portion control is tricky. I don't want him to go hungry, but it's also clear that he'll eat whatever we leave in the fridge now that he has discovered he can help himself. We know he will become frustrated if he opens the fridge and finds only kale and celery, so we are sure to leave a few fun foods he can have, in the correct portion, and then during the day we add more as needed.

We feel pretty good about our decisions of what to leave in the kitchen. Until the next morning, when I enter the kitchen and see an empty egg container on the counter. Confused, I started looking around for the eggs. Since Billy is in the bathroom, I have time to search the entire house.

After a pretty thorough search, I enlist the help of Jeff, Riley, and Jessica. We cannot find them—no shells, no eggs, nothing. I know the carton had five or six eggs in it.

Then, I hear the toilet flush multiple times.

"Oh boy," I say. "I think Billy just flushed all the eggs down the toilet."

Later, as I drive home from dropping off Riley, I pray for a miracle again. I pray every morning right after waking up for a miracle. I tell God that I have complete faith in Him, knowing that He can heal Billy. I believe this with all my heart. I have experienced His love, His peace, His strength given to me in so many storms, that I have no doubt that if He wanted to, He could instantly and fully heal Billy.

Then it really hits me again that I have no *reason* to hope, and I doubt on my own I could even continue to get out of bed in the morning since we do not know if Billy's challenges will ever end. But I have hope. I have hope that is renewed every day, and it certainly isn't hope generated by me. I could not live this way every day and have hope.

Sometimes I even have moments of a breakdown, when I think I cannot do it anymore. I get so tired and discouraged, I think and say I cannot do it anymore. But then I pray and open my Bible. Even when, or especially when I think that reading my Bible won't help, I move forward with praying and reading it. I find that even when I'm fighting my reluctance to read it, God reveals something to me that helps me tremendously. and even without a change in the circumstances, hope is poured into me, and in the next moment, I am again full of hope.

That's how I know it's hope from a source outside myself—God. Because there's no reason for it. "May the God of hope fill you with all joy and peace in believing, so that by the power of the Holy Spirit you may abound in hope" (Romans 15:13 ESV).

And this realization is followed by another—that I am growing and maturing spiritually. God is helping me to grow up. Although I will always be a child of His, with His help I can spend more time as a child and not a spoiled, fit-throwing toddler when He isn't helping Billy the way I want Him to.

Although He understands our human ways, He wants me to trust Him more and know that His ways are higher. "For as the heavens are higher than the earth, so are my ways higher than your ways, and my thoughts than your thoughts" (Isaiah 55:9 ESV).

CHAPTER 44

How Alarming

JEFF

I wake up abruptly out of a deep sleep.

As I register that there's a blaring noise coming from somewhere outside our room, Nancy jumps out of bed, looking wide awake.

"What's going on?" I somehow manage to mutter.

"It's the house alarm." She informs me, then adds "It's going off." As if that part weren't *blaringly* obvious.

I haul myself out of bed and stumble to the panel in the closet to see what set it off while Nancy grabs her cell phone and waits for the alarm company to call.

It takes my eyes a few seconds to focus, but when I finally blink away the fuzziness, I see that the panel shows it's Billy's bedroom window that is open.

I turn off the alarm, then go back out into the room and look at Nancy. "Billy's window is open."

Now that the obnoxious reverberation in our ears has subsided, the happy sound of Billy singing in his room is plain as day.

Relieved to know that there's no cause for concern, I cross back to the bed. "What time is it?"

She squints at her phone. "It's ten after two."

"Oh, has he been up all night?"

"I'm not sure." Her voice is a blend of concern and weariness. "He's been quiet for most of the night. I did hear him at around midnight, but I was hoping he was just talking in his sleep."

The sound of Billy clapping accentuates Nancy's comment. "But, clearly . . ." I huff out a chuckle. ". . . he is up"

After resetting the alarm and explaining the situation to the alarm company, we settle back into bed, all while listening to Billy run around his room singing "Old McDonald."

Nancy tosses me a look. "Did you sing that with him last night?"

"Yes, I did. He was having a great time doing the animal noises with me." I let out a little *moo* that dissolves into a weak attempt at a laugh. Well, it was funny then, but now, I guess it's not that funny.

While sitting silently in bed, waiting for the adrenaline rush to subside, I hold Nancy's hand. I pray for three things: *God, please help Billy calm down; God, please help my wife to calm down and be able to sleep; and please God, don't let me say anything dumb in my effort to fix this situation.*

In the past, I would have jumped right into fix-it mode. I would have said, "You know we can bypass Billy's window at night so he can't set the alarm off." But I now know that when we are in the middle of a rough situation, it is not the time to offer suggestions on how to fix it. Instead, I pray some more and ask God to have mercy on us.

Please, Lord. Calm us down.

As I start to drift off to sleep, I thank God for helping me. I'm also very grateful to be retired so I don't have to rush off to work in a few hours. I realize how much He has helped me to focus on being there for my wife and my family, in ways that truly help. He has relieved me of feeling the need to fix everything. He has shown me that it is really His job, in His timing. He reminds me of all I can do that helps relieve Nancy's burden—running errands, picking up groceries, doing laundry or dishes, and cooking. All the things I can do to lighten the workload.

I know that Nancy is a very light sleeper. Knowing she will most likely be awake for the rest of the night, I prepare my mind for the day ahead of us by asking God to keep me focused on how best to provide real help.

CHAPTER 45

I Won't Let You Down

NANCY

It has been almost twenty-one years since Billy was born and almost nineteen years since his autism diagnosis. I remember it as clearly as if it happened yesterday. I remember the look of the office, the smell of the new carpet, the face of the pediatrician as she told me, "Your son has pervasive developmental disorder."

Although my head spun and I felt like running from the room, I wanted answers from her. "What do we do?" I asked.

"Spend time with him. Just play with him and spend time with him."

"We already do that. What else?" I needed more from her, and all she could tell me was to spend time with him while handing me the cards for a speech therapist and occupational therapist.

As we drove home, I watched Billy in the rearview mirror. *We can do this, little boy. I won't let you down.* I thought about the previous two years with him, about how much I love being his mom, and about how completely head over heels I am for my sweet Billy. As tears rolled down my face, I thought about my pregnancy. I had read every book on child development and raising children I could get my hands on. I was super excited even though through over half my pregnancy I was so sick that I could rarely leave the house.

The first months after Billy's birth were more challenging than I'd imagined, but the advice I received was "Hang in there. It gets easier."

When I endured sleepless nights, they really were sleepless. At age two, Billy still only slept for two hours at a time, and then he would wake up and need to be rocked back to sleep. Although I would try to get to sleep again as quickly as possible, I had at the most an hour and a half before I would be up again.

Nevertheless, even with waking every hour during the night for either feeding or easing his upset stomach, I loved being Billy's mommy.

I look back at those first couple of years with incredible joy even though I was blurry-eyed through it all. We could sit and look into each other's eyes for hours, and I adored him then like I still do.

Now Billy is twenty-one, and we have to try and try again when it comes to his protocols. And we don't know what to do.

Although we have tried many treatments for PANDAS, the only thing that has proven successful for Billy is homeopathy. With homeopathy remedies, he's been able to return to some of the activities he enjoys, like acting out his favorite scenes from shows he likes, playing musical toys, and singing songs. I hoped he would eventually be able to resume his music therapy and his horseback riding therapy. We are sure that even though every three steps he moves forward will be followed by one step back, we are still going in the right direction.

However, since the beginning of 2017, each single step forward is followed immediately by a step back.

How do people do things like this without the hope of Jesus?

CHAPTER 46

Answered Prayers

NANCY

After a very rough night, with Billy waking up multiple times, I feel like I'm at my wit's end. I dash into our master bathroom and shut the door. Turning around to gaze at but then avoid my disheveled reflection in the mirror, I take some deep breaths, then blurt out in a voice that's just short of yelling, "When, God? When are You going to use this situation for our good?"

I know that verse well. "And we know that in all things God works for the good of those who love Him, and have been called according to His purpose" (Romans 8:28).

I then realize that I'm once again mad at God, and I know I *should* stop, but I'm too upset.

After another minute of ranting out loud in the Lord's general direction, I stop and lean against the counter. I've made a bad habit of doing this. When things are really unbearable, like they are today, I go to a room where Billy can't hear me—either the garage or the master bathroom—and loudly recite those verses to God. I tell Him that He isn't doing His part. I feel hurt and angry.

The other verse I often recite is "Trust in the Lord with *all* your heart and lean not on your understanding, but in *all* your ways acknowledge Him, and He will direct your paths" (Proverbs 3:5–6, emphasis mine). I've committed both verses to memory. Living them out is what's difficult. It's tough when my child is sick and not doing well. I want solutions, and I want them now.

On days like today, it's difficult to remember life before Billy became so sick. When we watch the videos from our trips or I run into someone I haven't seen in years, I'm reminded that we used to have a more normal life.

It has been quite a process and is still a daily process to surrender to God's plan. There were many days, months, and years when I searched for the answer(s). I thought if I just worked harder, prayed harder, did something better, Billy would get well.

I grab a washcloth from the rack, run some cold water over it, and rest it on the back of my neck. The cold is jolting but comforts and calms me nonetheless.

After exhausting myself with my ranting, I finally turn fully to prayer. "Lord . . ." My voice is softer now, a reasonable volume that reflects my worn-out spirit. "Please give me the strength I need to continue through this day. To be there for Billy and the rest of my family. I trust that You have a purpose in this, God, even though I can't see it."

I pause, silently sobbing. But in that moment, I sense something. A feeling of peace washes over me. Then the thought that this is God's plan. I don't understand it. I don't like it. But I know that He *will* use this for His glory, and I need to be faithful and patient while it plays out.

It's not easy, but in that moment, I feel a reassurance that as difficult as things are, God is in it.

I have to remember, especially on the hard days like today, that I need to turn to Him.

My part is to trust Him, obey Him, and be patient. He knows my pain, and He cares. The sad part is that even though I know this, I have complete toddler meltdowns at times. That might not change, but I'll do my best.

I know that God isn't looking for perfection in His children. He knows me. He understands my limitations. I think of something Pastor David Jeremiah said during a Sunday message: being a Christian is falling down, getting up, falling down, getting up . . . all the way to heaven.

Like any good parent, God guides me using the Bible and His Holy Spirit. He loves me unconditionally. He wants me to stay with Him and hold His hand so I don't have to struggle as much.

I gain perspective in remembering *all* the times He has answered my prayers clearly and quickly. It helps me know that although He could heal Billy at this moment, He must have a reason why He hasn't, at least not yet. My job is to simply live out my day trusting Him and His plan.

When I remind myself that God is our heavenly *Father*, it helps my perspective. Jeff and I have faced many situations where one of our kids wanted to do something that we knew was not in their best interests. No matter how many chores they do, how much begging, pleading, promising, we will not allow it because it's not for their best.

In the same way, I tell myself, I need to accept that for whatever reason, it's not God's plan to heal Billy right now. No amount of pleading or pouting will change that. Instead, I do my best to follow His plan, the plan where I continue to pray, read, and memorize His Word; thank Him for the many blessings we have; and rely on Him to get me through each moment. If I can keep reminding myself of this, maybe I can at least cut back on my meltdowns.

Feeling renewed, I open the bathroom door and creep out into the bedroom. Not hearing any sounds from the rest of the house, I peer into the hallway. Billy's door is closed, so I know he's still in there.

Breathing a sigh of relief, I go back into my room and pull up a blog I read a few days ago. I love the way Dr. David Jeremiah talks about prayer, and I read again the teaching that has helped me with my attitude.

When we're under pressure, our tendency is to rush into His presence with our list of needs without even saying "hello" to the Lord: "God, I need this, this, this, this, and this. And, I need it now, and tomorrow, and the next day. If You could go ahead and get it done ahead of time, that would be even better."[6]

Real prayer, I have discovered, is a lifestyle of love for the Lord. Rushing into His presence with my laundry list of needs without pausing to truly focus on Him can depress me more than if I hadn't prayed at all!

On Billy's pain-free days, I can easily get focused on the tasks at hand and forget about God and prayer. While today's a difficult day, maybe I can use it to remind myself to pray on Billy's next pain-free day. But how will I remember to do that?

Heaving a sigh, I kneel to put the book away. My eye latches on to my phone, and the thought hits me like a jolt of caffeine. My phone calendar. Can it be that simple? Can I set reminders to pray like I set reminders for other things I want to accomplish?

With renewed energy, I plop myself onto the bed and start typing like crazy. Reminders to pray.

It feels good. Like making little promises to God.

---

6   David Jeremiah, "7 Prayers for Inner Peace," David Jeremiah Blog. https://davidjeremi-ah.blog/7-prayers-for-inner-peace/.

CHAPTER 47

Trusting, Finally

NANCY

A month ago—January of 2020—Billy turned twenty-two. I keep hoping . . . praying . . . that things will get easier. But tonight, once again, Billy goes to bed late. I'm way too tired to do much, so I decide to look for some new toys or books on eBay. Billy tends to go through toys pretty quickly. Since he enjoys playing with his animal or mermaid toys in the bath, he recently decided that when he takes a shower, he should have toys in there as well. However, since there are no toys in the shower, he created his own fun. Apparently, emptying Mom's shampoo bottle to see the bubbles seems fun.

After that, he has fun watching the bar of soap dissolve under the stream of water. Then, once finished with those "toys," he jumps out and grabs the roll of toilet paper. Jackpot! It dissolves well and blocks the drain. He laughs as the shampoo bubble water rises around his ankles.

As I search for toys that might work in the shower, I find some puzzles he may like. Most of his puzzles are pretty damaged, and when I find some Barney puzzles, I'm pretty excited. However, there is a problem: the puzzles are all ten to fifteen pieces. Billy could do those in just a few minutes. He needs puzzles with more pieces. I keep searching until it dawns on me. There are no Barney puzzles with fifty pieces, since Barney is for small children, not someone twenty-two years old. *Geez. I am tired!*

I'm grateful when Billy is finally in bed at 10:15 and not later. But at 1:15 a.m., I wake up to the sound of laughter. Then as I step into the hallway, I hear some other happy noises. I tiptoe closer to Billy's door to listen, hoping he's talking in his sleep.

But the rustle of his ball pit tells me that he is up. Being careful not to wake Jeff, I scoot back to bed to pray. In the past, my prayers would have simply been begging God to help him sleep. But now, instead, I thank God.

I thank Him that Billy sounds happy instead of mad. I thank God that Billy is quiet enough not to wake up others. Most of all, I thank God that even if Billy does not go back to sleep (if he ever was asleep to begin with), I know that God will get us through. Because God has gotten us through every time.

It hasn't been easy—yes, I have often been extremely tired—but He always gets us through. So as much as I would have rolled my eyes years ago at anyone who suggested thanking Him, I do it now with all sincerity.

Three hours later, Billy is quiet, and I can finally doze off. Until 6:30, when Billy is up again. I don't know if he slept in or if he's been awake since his usual time but stayed in his room and kept quiet. I pray for strength and for an easy day with my son.

Once I'm up, Billy emerges from his room as happy as he would be after a full night's sleep. How is this possible? I don't know, other than I know that with God, all things are possible, like it says in Matthew 19:26.

In this moment, I recall that, especially after Billy's autism diagnosis so many years ago, people would often say, "God has a plan here" or "Trust God to work it all out." I didn't know how to respond to these statements. I wish I had asked, How do I do that? Instead I thought, *Wow, you are pretty delusional, aren't you?* Or *Wow, silly girl. Yeah, okay, I will just trust God*, while rolling my eyes internally. What I thought I knew about God at that time was that He expected me to be really good, go to church often, and just hope for heaven one day.

So the thought that God had some plan for me now—well, that just sounded silly.

Not anymore. Today Billy is happy when he should be exhausted. And that is just a gift from my heavenly Father, His plan for our day. I'm grateful.

As we move into fall, so many things are out of control in our world.

Since the pandemic hit in March, daily life is more confusing. I know many people have it much more difficult than our family does. I cannot imagine living in one of the cities where rioting, looting, and violence are a daily occurrence. Every day as I deal with Billy, I think about how uncertain the future is for so many.

Billy is going through a very rough time, but thankfully, because of his level of functioning, he has no idea what's taking place in our world. He enjoys being home, so avoiding going out hasn't affected him. He would never understand the need for wearing a mask. Because of his sensory issues, he would not be able to tolerate a mask. He would completely lose it if he ever saw any of us in a mask. It would not make any sense to him at all.

Seven years ago, we put the Bible verse Romans 12:12 on our bedroom wall: "Be joyful in hope, patient in affliction, faithful in prayer." Every morning I read it and pray that today will be the day God will heal Billy of his PANDAS. Some days I'm angry. I feel that since I am being patient in affliction and faithful in praying and certainly joyful knowing that one day we would spend eternity in heaven, God should just go ahead and heal Billy.

Seven years is a long time. It's a long time to endure. It's a long time to pray for something and wait and wait and wait.

I remind myself of the faithful servants of God who spent years waiting. Like Moses, and also Joseph, who spent years in prison, or the apostle Paul, who after his miraculous conversion sometimes spent years in prison.

I cannot say that I've been all that trusting during these seven years. It's not that I don't believe God is capable. There is never a morning that I do not wake up and think that today may be the day. I trust fully in God's ability to restore Billy's mind and body. It's mostly that I'm upset knowing that He can heal yet chooses not to. My mind goes to places like *If He really loved me, He would fix this situation* or *What am I doing wrong?* Of course, I could come up with many things I'm doing wrong—not praying enough, not reading my Bible enough, not trusting enough, not being patient enough, not putting out enough prayer requests, fighting against the life He has placed me in . . .

I remind myself of Isaiah 55:8: "'For My thoughts are not your thoughts, neither are your ways My ways,' declares the Lord."

But sometimes, even more often than not, I like my way. Like how I like to lead when I dance. It's ironic since I don't dance much and am not a good dancer. What is even more ironic is that I don't even realize I'm leading until the person I am dancing with tells me. To make things even worse, even after being told, I can't stop leading.

It's like giving a toddler the map and asking her to direct you to your destination.

I know God is in control. I know He has a plan, and it's a well-developed, amazing plan, yet I want to take the lead. Even though I know that once I'm out in front of God, messing up, I'll get angry at Him for how things are going.

And I know it's my choice. I must choose His way—even though His way is counterintuitive to everything I've learned about getting things done.

The problem I've run into time and time again with Billy and his health issues is that none of my plans work. They are well-researched plans. Many times, I think I have found the perfect solution. Many times, however, I run around and around in circles. I never give up though, but it's exhausting.

Then there are those times when, in utter despair, I give up and really cry out to God for help.

What I want to be able to do is turn to Him first. Let Him lead. I have done this successfully a few times, and I'm amazed at how He places the answers in front of me, right in front of me, usually from multiple sources to give me the reassurance that I am on the right track. He does this without all my effort.

A perfect example of this is how we found one of Billy's doctors when searching for a PANDAS expert. After reviewing a list that contained many names and thinking that I might have to research every single one to find the right one, I put the list at the top of my to-do stack. After a quick lunch, I sat down to begin researching, and instead of diving in, I prayed. I asked God to make it clear to me.

At this point, I was still thinking I would have to research all options, and then God would help me choose. Instead, one name jumped out from the parent group of recommendations. Then I looked at another website, and there it was—the same doctor's name again. Then, just to be sure I was getting the message, another mom I know posted about this particular doctor. I prayed again, asking God, Is this the one? And He gave me the peace to know, *Yes, this is the doctor.* With God leading (because I allowed Him to), my struggling and researching for days or weeks was completed in less than an hour. What an amazing God we have.

I love those times so much. But all too often I revert right back to trying to take the lead again. Knowing this about myself, I have to make the decision each morning and then again multiple times a day to put Him first. It can be as simple as praying a prayer that includes *Lord, please don't let me lead* or *Lord, help me see this situation how You see it* or *Lord, help me to choose the path You want to lead me down.*

Most of all, it is choosing to live out the verse "Be still, and know that I am God" (Psalm 46:10). The challenge in this verse for me is to be still in my mind. My mind will race with ideas, especially ideas on how God might get done what I would like done. So I have to recite this verse until my mind quiets enough to let God be God.

CHAPTER 48

For Better or Worse

JEFF

It's 7:20 a.m., and I'm sitting on the couch, with a *Mr. Rogers* episode on the TV screen all set to play. Nancy has just set two bowls of scrambled eggs on the coffee table—one for me and one for Billy. She gives me a kiss on the cheek and heads to the dining room for her morning Bible reading time.

I look up as Billy enters the room. "You ready, buddy?"

The smile on his face says it all. He throws himself down next to me, and I grab the remote and hit Play.

We've seen this episode a dozen times, but we don't care. The important thing for me is spending time with my boy, having breakfast in "the neighborhood" with Mr. Rogers. When this episode ends, Billy will most likely want to watch *Winnie the Pooh*.

This has become our daily routine, a routine that I've grown to treasure.

Once our shows are over, I pick up our dishes, and Jessica joins Billy on the couch. While I clean up, I can't help but smile at the sound of the two of them, listening to music and playing with stuffed animals. They've developed their own sweet relationship over the years too.

By the time I've finished up in the kitchen, Billy has gone upstairs, along with Nancy. I go up too, to check on email and get on with my day. I see that Billy's had a shower, and he's now in his swing—we have a big hammock-style therapy swing that hangs in our master bedroom. It's comforting having him there.

The joy I see in him while he watches TV, jumps on the trampoline, and sings and dances along to the songs fills me with joy. Sometimes we hold hands and dance, and sometimes we spin around in circles for the whole song, or as much as I can without getting too dizzy. The fact that he enjoys these simple shows so much at twenty-four-years old leaves me feeling a deep sense of joy. It is hard to imagine, I know, but this brings me a sense of satisfaction that is difficult to describe.

Billy and I have come a long way in our relationship. Twelve years ago, right after Nancy and I married, my interactions with Billy were limited, but now he trusts me and enjoys my friendship—there isn't anything I wouldn't do for him. I always liked him, and I knew he was part of the package with marrying Nancy, but now my love for Billy is so deep that I cannot imagine my life without him.

Friends have asked me, given how hard things are with Billy, if I have ever just considered leaving. The answer is no, I have not considered leaving. Not only do I love what I'm doing even though it's hard, I also took vows, vows that included "for better or worse." I knew what I was doing when I took these vows. I had been through the worst with my wife passing away, so I knew exactly what I was saying when I vowed to be here.

I know now that people who are like Billy, people with special needs to the extent he has, are often overlooked in our world. I wish they weren't. I wish more people could experience the joy that comes through them. I am so blessed, and I do not know of anything that provides this same level of knowing, just knowing that I make a difference in Billy's world.

The kid who cannot give me anything gives me everything.

As Jesus said in Matthew 22:37–39 (undoubtedly the two greatest commandments): "Love the Lord your God with all your heart and with all your soul and with all your mind. This is the first and greatest commandment. And the second is like it: Love your neighbor as yourself." Nancy and Billy are my closest "neighbors," and my life revolves around the Lord and those two. I wouldn't have it any other way. God gave me an opportunity, and I daily try to honor it, thanking God for both of them.

CHAPTER 49

Happy(ish) Ending

NANCY

It's very early on Sunday morning. I hear Billy rustling around in his room. As I slip out of bed, Jeff whispers to me, "What time is it?"

I yawn out an answer. "Three forty-five."

As I start the coffee, which is on the bedside table, Jeff rolls over and says, "What am I doing sleeping this late on a Sunday? I'm so lazy. I gotta get up."

I look at him, and the two of us just start cracking up.

I am so blessed. God has blessed me with the best husband ever. While I'm making coffee, I hear Billy's bedroom door open.

He sounds really happy, talking about Elmo and Big Bird. I make a mental note to find his *Sesame Street* books and music to fill his afternoon.

I take a snack and a cup of water to him. He takes them, then closes his door.

By the time I make it back to our room, Jeff has poured the coffee. We settle back into bed with our coffee mugs on our nightstands and begin to discuss the plans for the day.

"Did I tell you that I talked to Colin yesterday?" Jeff takes a sip of the coffee and makes an *mmm* sound.

"No." I lean back against my pillow, grateful for its plushness. "How's he doing?"

"He's good. Said he might move to Colorado next year, but he isn't sure."

That reminds me, I need to check in with Riley. I think her graduation is early May, but I really need to get the date so we can work on respite care unless Gia is available for Billy that day.

"Oh, I forgot to tell you," I say. "Jessica is looking into a new job at the preschool."

"That's great! She did really like her time volunteering there."

Just then, we hear laughter coming from Billy's room. Then we hear the sound of Mr. Rogers's voice coming from his portable DVD player. I smile, thinking about how much Billy loves the simple things.

By midmorning, we are in full swing, enjoying our caffeine energy. I realize it's time for Billy's breakfast and bath.

Ten minutes later, I place his breakfast sandwich on a tray outside his door. I slide a note under his door to let him know it's time to eat. He is going through a phase where he doesn't like to be interrupted, and with notes under his door, he knows what's next but can also open the door when he is ready. This reduces his anxiety. He has some control over his day.

No sooner do I make it back to our room than he comes storming into our room, making his way to the bathroom with his breakfast sandwich in his hand. He is clearly upset.

Jeff and I look at each other with wide eyes. Why is he so upset?

Fortunately, I have his bath water ready. As Billy jumps into the bath while eating his sandwich, I retrieve the note from where he left it next to the sink. I realize my mistake. Instead of writing "first food, and then bath" on his note, I had hurriedly written "food and bath."

So there he is in the bath with his food.

Billy calms down quickly in the tub, finishes his sandwich, and begins playing with his toys. Jeff and I crack up at how the lack of a couple of words—*first* food, and *then* bath—makes all the difference. In the future, I'm pretty sure I will remember to pay close attention to the notes I slide under his door.

With Billy settled in the bath, we jump into action. We call this our "NASCAR pit crew time." We know we must move quickly to get Billy's room cleaned up and ready for his afternoon. Since we do not have any appointments today, he will want to play in there without being disturbed. We quickly strip and remake his bed, clean up any dishes, put his books into neat piles, move out some toys, and replace them with toys he hasn't seen in a while.

Once Billy is clean, I get him dressed and then hand him the schedule of today's activities, which I have taped to a cardboard backing so it will withstand him carrying it around all day:

1. Books
2. Music time
3. Lunch and Mr. Rogers and Winnie the Pooh with Daddy
4. Swing and trampoline
5. Movie
6. Books
7. Dinner and playtime with Mommy and Daddy
8. Music
9. Bedtime

After he completes each activity, we cross it off the list. I'm careful to leave a few blank spaces for those days when he hurries through the list. He has no concept of telling time, so there are times when we need to speed up or slow down by adding or eliminating something.

We have a very simple life now. Every day, we pray for complete healing for Billy, if not from his autism, then from PANDAS. And almost every day, we wonder why God's answer seems to be *Not now.*

In spite of this, we know He's always with us even in the most difficult times when we don't see the answer to our prayers. We know we are living out God's plans for our lives, and that brings us peace.

Incredible peace.

CHAPTER 50

Holding His Hand

NANCY

This is the chapter I don't want to write but need to. Throughout this process, I have repeatedly told God that I cannot continue to write this book. What does God do in response? He puts it on my heart to write about everything I don't want to write about.

I would love to report that every morning I wake up eager to pray and see what God has in store for me. Some mornings I do wake up that way, but others, I wake up dreading the day and finding it hard to pray. In fact, I have even come to the point where I have told God that I cannot continue to pray for healing for Billy. It is just too hard to continue to pray for something year after year that is just not happening. However, I find that even after saying that to God, He does not let me stop praying for Billy's healing. I find myself praying for Billy's healing even when I don't want to. That can only come from the work of the Holy Spirit.

I would like to tell you that when the hard days happen, I just pray and trust God. Instead, I need to tell you that some days I fall apart. When Billy is struggling and I cannot figure out how to help him, I sometimes lose it.

I want more from God than I'm getting (or so I think), and when God doesn't come through, I'm angry. I'm sad, I feel abandoned, and I'm more than happy to get impatient with my husband. In those moments, I begin to think things like *Well, now I've done it. God will completely turn His back on me now.* I mean, why wouldn't He? I would. If someone completely melted down like I do, I wouldn't want to be around them.

But then I remember that Jesus, as my Savior, intervenes on my behalf. He paid the price so I can be forgiven by God, both now and for eternity. That truth soothes me and brings me back to where I need to be. Sometimes it's several times a day. My prayer throughout the day is often *Oh, God, forgive me and help me.*

We already know there is no one-size-fits-all, but God really perfects it by customizing His approach with me—He meets me exactly where I am. I think back on the day of Keith's surgery when I had no idea about the Bible or who Jesus really is. God met me exactly where I was and provided me with peace.

Twenty years later, now that I know more about Him, He requires more of me—more patience and more trusting Him based on His Word and not what I'm seeing or feeling.

When I just cannot make sense of what we are going through, my go-to verse is Isaiah 55:9: "As the heavens are higher than the earth, so are My ways higher than your ways and My thoughts than your thoughts."

When I feel like I just cannot make it through a challenging time, Isaiah 43:2 comforts me: "When you pass through the waters, I will be with you; and when you pass through the rivers, they will not sweep over you. When you walk through the fire, you will not be burned; the flames will not set you ablaze."

I may feel like I'm on my own and I'm drowning or burning, but God says otherwise. He knows my situation, and He says I will not drown or be burned, and since He is God, He knows. I have to choose Him by reciting this verse, sometimes over and over. I will tell Him that I feel like I am drowning. I feel like this will never end, and I'm not going to be able to overcome this . . . but He says otherwise, and He is way wiser than I am.

As I write this, in addition to Billy's ongoing struggles, we also have the world struggles to deal with, so every day I make the choice (sometimes moment by moment) to remember and call to mind His promises. I also make sure that when I pray, I thank Him for the many blessings. Even if it's a rough day and the blessings are barely visible, they are there, and when I thank Him, it helps refocus my mind on how good He is, even if He does not answer my prayers as quickly as I would like.

When I think I cannot go on, I look back at what He has done for me. Just this morning the Lord reminded me about the times I now look back on, and I thought, *Wow, how did I make it through that?* Well, I made it through that because He did the heavy lifting. At the time, I thought it was all me, but looking back I can see it was all Him.

It's important to me now to grab hold of His hand each morning and hold on tight. When things get rough and I begin falling apart, running around in circles, trying to make sense of it all, and trying to fix things only to see them crumble, I now run back and open my Bible as a way of grabbing His hand again. While holding His hand, he brings to mind the Scripture I need to refocus and get a grip.

Growing in faith means increasing my dependence on Him and recognizing my need at a deeper level each day. It is becoming less about me striving (although if I'm not careful, I backslide into that thinking) to become anything and more about turning it over to Him. That is spiritual growth.

I used to think that I would arrive at some kind of spiritual wholeness that would allow me to need less from God on a daily basis. It's actually the opposite—spiritual wholeness only comes from being fully dependent on Him and holding His hand as tight as I can.

Thank you for reading *Holding His Hand.*

Please help other readers find this book by leaving an honest review on Amazon, Goodreads, and wherever you shop for books online.

Acknowledgments

Thank you to our family and friends who supported us and provided help during our most challenging times. You know who you are. To our praying friends; Gia, Sherry, Anne, Kellie, Brooke, and Sara. Thank you for praying every time I sent you a text!

A very special thank-you to Gia. You know what this life is like (because you live it too). Every step of the way, you provided help and encouragement.

A very special thank-you to Sherry. Your encouragement, prayers and guidance mean so much.

An extra special thank-you to Noah and Lauren for making lemonade out of some pretty bitter lemons.

Thank you to Lesley for your incredible insight and help in turning our story into what it needed to be.

Additional thank-you to Jack Hibbs, J.D. Farag, and David Jeremiah for faithfully teaching truth.

Resources

With so much deception and censorship in our world today, we wanted to give some helpful resources:

Books by Ray Stedman
Books by Charles Stanley
Real Life with Jack Hibbs
J.D. Farag.org
Dr. David Jeremiah.org
JB Hixson.org or notbyworks.org